The Shakespeare Handbooks

THE SHAKESPEARE HANDBOOKS

Series Editor: John Russell Brown

PUBLISHED

FORTHCOMING

The Shakespeare Handbooks

A Midsummer Night's Dream

Martin White

palgrave
macmillan

First published 2009 by
PALGRAVE MACMILLAN

Palgrave Macmillan in the UK is an imprint of Macmillan Publishers Limited, registered in England, company number 785998, of Houndmills, Basingstoke, Hampshire RG21 6XS.

Palgrave Macmillan in the US is a division of St Martin's Press LLC, 175 Fifth Avenue, New York, NY 10010.

Palgrave Macmillan is the global academic imprint of the above companies and has companies and representatives throughout the world.

Palgrave® and Macmillan® are registered trademarks in the United States, the United Kingdom, Europe and other countries.

ISBN-13: 978–1–4039–4537–2 hardback
ISBN-10: 1–4039–4537–3 hardback
ISBN-13: 978–1–4039–4538–9 paperback
ISBN-10: 1–4039–4538–1 paperback

This book is printed on paper suitable for recycling and made from fully managed and sustained forest sources. Logging, pulping and manufacturing processes are expected to conform to the environmental regulations of the country of origin.

A catalogue record for this book is available from the British Library.

Library of Congress Cataloging-in-Publication Data

White, Martin, 1947–
        A midsummer night's dream / Martin White.
            p. cm.—(The Shakespeare handbooks)
        Includes bibliographical references and index.
        ISBN-13: 978–1–4039–4537–2 (hbk. : alk. paper)
        ISBN-10: 1–4039–4537–3 (hbk. : alk. paper)
        ISBN-13: 978–1–4039–4538–9 (pbk. : alk. paper)
        ISBN-10: 1–4039–4538–1 (pbk. : alk. paper)
        1. Shakespeare, William, 1564–1616. Midsummer night's dream –
Handbooks, manuals, etc. 2. Shakespeare, William, 1564–1616 – Stage history.
3. Shakespeare, William, 1564–1616 – Film and video adaptations. I. Title.

PR2827.W47 2009
822.3'3—dc22   2008039123

10 9 8 7 6 5 4 3 2 1
18 17 16 15 14 13 12 11 10 09

Printed and bound in China

For Philip and Kate, and everyone else on that tour of Germany in 1967

Contents

General Editor's Preface

The Shakespeare Handbooks provide an innovative way of studying the plays in performance. The commentaries, which are their core feature, enable a reader to envisage the words of a text unfurling in performance, involving actions and meanings not readily perceived except in rehearsal or performance. The aim is to present the plays in the environment for which they were written and to offer an experience as close as possible to an audience's progressive experience of a production.

While each book has the same range of contents, their authors have been encouraged to shape them according to their own critical and scholarly understanding and their first-hand experience of theatre practice. The various chapters are designed to complement the commentaries: the cultural context of each play is presented together with quotations from original sources; the authority of its text or texts is considered with what is known of the earliest performances; key performances and productions of its subsequent stage history are both described and compared. The aim in all this has been to help readers to develop their own informed and imaginative view of a play in ways that supplement the provision of standard editions and are more user-friendly than detailed stage histories or collections of criticism from diverse sources.

Further volumes are in preparation so that, within a few years, the Shakespeare Handbooks will be available for all the plays that are frequently performed and studied.

John Russell Brown

Preface

Like many who will read this book I have seen a great number of professional productions on *A Midsummer Night's Dream*, performed in it myself as a student (at university, followed by a tour of Germany, as Lysander) and seen my son play both Theseus and Demetrius in school productions. As a university teacher I have often discussed it with my students (especially while I've been working on this book) and benefited from their ideas, and I have enjoyed and learnt from the wealth of critical opinion on the play that exists. I need to thank all those involved in these experiences for the different insights each has provided, even though I'm not always sure who was responsible for what. More specifically, I am grateful to John Russell Brown, first for inviting me to contribute to his series and then continuing to take a close and always stimulating interest in the book's progress. Jo Elsworth and Rachel Hassall at the University of Bristol Theatre Collection were their usual helpful selves, especially with access to the Herbert Beerbohm Tree archive, and my colleague Catherine Hindson answered a number of my queries about Tree and his work. Perdita Davidson kindly read and commented on draft material and, as always, my partner Alison Steele was able to sustain an interest in the book despite its long stay in our house.

Martin White

1 The Text and Early Performances

Date

We cannot know for certain when Shakespeare wrote *A Midsummer Night's Dream*, but it was well-enough known by 1598 for Francis Meres to include it in his commonplace book, *Palladis Tamia: Wit's Treasury*, as an example of the playwright's 'excellence' in writing comedies. The play was not published until 1600, so Meres' comments not only reflect its success on stage, but also set the latest possible date for its composition. It is generally agreed that the maturity of style in the writing and control of the dramatic and theatrical structure suggest the play should be placed at the end of the sequence of comedies Shakespeare wrote in the 1590s: *The Two Gentlemen of Verona*, *The Taming of the Shrew*, *The Comedy of Errors* and *Love's Labour's Lost* (which themselves cannot be firmly dated). Opinions differ on whether *Romeo and Juliet* (which was published in 1597) preceded or followed the comedy, but I have taken the view that the tragedy is the earlier play.

A reference to an entertainment at the Scottish court in 1594, when a plan for a chariot to be pulled in by a lion was changed at the last minute 'because his presence might have brought some fear to the nearest, or that the lights and torches might have commoved his tameness', has been used to set the earliest date.

Titania's speech (II.i.81–117) is often seen as referring to the unusually and disastrously wet summers between 1594 and 1597, and her comments about uncommonly fine winters to the mild and sunny conditions in February 1596. Others have suggested that the play also makes reference, through the presence of its group of artisans, to social upheaval, including disturbances (one led by a weaver) in the Midsummer period of 1595 (Patterson 1989, pp. 52–72; Williams 1995) and the clear signs of severe economic distress being felt by working people.

Taking all this into account, it seems reasonable to set the date of composition around 1595–6.

Publication

A Midsummer Night's Dream presents fewer textual problems than probably any other Shakespeare play, and there is general consensus over the solutions to what problems there are (see Holland's edition, 1994, pp. 112–17 for a good summary). The play was first published, in quarto (Q1), in 1600, with a title page announcing that it had been 'sundry times publicly acted by the Right Honourable the Lord Chamberlain his Servants' – the Lord Chamberlain's Men as the company is more commonly known. (The company became the King's Men on 19 May 1603 when King James took them under his own patronage, so securing their survival and success.) The printer probably worked from a manuscript in Shakespeare's own handwriting, containing the changes and corrections he made while composing the play. Q1 occasionally has different speech headings for the same character – Theseus and Hippolyta become 'Duke' and 'Dutch' midway through Act V, for example – and a number of stage directions are incomplete and at times inconsistent or unclear, such as the inclusion of Helena in the entry at I.i.19, although she does not speak (and may well not enter) until line 179. A second quarto (Q2) followed in 1619 (with a false date of 1600 on the title page), which is basically a reprinting of Q1, with only minor differences. The play was included in the First Folio (F1), the collected edition of Shakespeare's plays compiled after his death by his former colleagues, John Heminge and Henry Condell, and published in 1623. The Folio text (which, unlike either quarto, is divided into five acts) appears to have been printed from Q2, but in some instances provides answers to misprints in Q1. Other changes in F1, which may derive from the compositor referring to a prompt copy – such as the assigning of Philostrate's speeches in Act V to Egeus – are more significant in terms of the play in performance and so may be of particular interest to actors and directors, and will be raised at relevant points in the Commentary. F1 also contains examples of what Gurr and Ichikawa call 'duplicated stage directions' (2000, p. 117). In III.i, for example, F1 adds *Enter Puck* at III.i.49, but also retains Q2's *Enter Robin* at line 70 in the scene. (Modern editions vary in how they handle this apparent discrepancy: the 2005 Penguin edition text that I have used throughout this book selects just the later entry, the Oxford the earlier one.) In IV.i, F1 retains Q2's entry for Oberon at the start of the scene, but also gives the character a later entry at line 44. These may simply be errors on the printer's part, but Gurr and Ichikawa raise the possibility that in each case 'the two entries may work differently, the first indicating the arrival and the second the action of coming forward' to intervene in the scene (2000, p. 118).

First performances

Dating the first *performances* of an early modern play (which usually followed soon after its completion by the author and a short – by our standards – rehearsal period: see White 1998, pp. 28–33) is often more difficult than establishing the date of composition. Although both quartos refer to public performances, the only specific references to early performances are in private venues: before King James at Hampton Court on 1 January 1604 (if it is indeed the same as the 'play of Robin good-fellowe' in the records), in 1630, again at Hampton Court for Charles I, and in 1631, probably in Buckden Palace near Huntingdon, the residence of John Williams, the Lord Bishop of Lincoln. Some critics, however, have argued strongly that the company first staged the play privately at (even that it was specifically commissioned for) an aristocratic wedding. Some 11 weddings have been put forward, of which the most likely is the marriage of Elizabeth Carey – named after her godmother, Queen Elizabeth, and known to have had an interest in dreams – to Thomas Berkeley, celebrated in London on the nineteenth of that unusually sunny February of 1596. Both families had interests in plays and playing: the Berkeleys had their own troupe of players while, more significantly, the bride's grandfather and, later, her father, were patrons of the Lord Chamberlain's Men, and her father possibly commissioned *The Merry Wives of Windsor* (another play that features fairies). The Careys' London home was in Blackfriars, and, as the local church records make no mention of their daughter's marriage, it probably took place in the family's private chapel at their home.

The play's reference to a 'fair vestal thronèd by the west' (II.i.158) in a speech that appears to recall directly an entertainment presented to the queen (see Chapter 3, pp. 92–4), and redolent (as is the play) with the moon imagery associated with Elizabeth, may well be a compliment to the Virgin Queen. Harold Bloom calls the speech 'Shakespeare's largest and most direct tribute to his monarch during her lifetime' (1999, p. 159), though 'the precise nature of the compliment is so elusive that it took nearly 20 closely printed pages in the Variorum edition to elucidate all the possible interpretations of it that were put forward in the eighteenth and nineteenth centuries alone' (Bate 1997, p. 218). The Carey family were the Queen's closest living relatives: the mother of the bride's grandfather, Henry Carey, was Mary Boleyn, Anne's sister, which made him Queen Elizabeth's first cousin or even possibly her half-brother, as Mary had been Henry VIII's mistress before Anne. However, the suggestion that the Queen – who was in residence at her palace in Richmond on that day – was herself a guest at the wedding, without her presence being recorded, is less likely to be true.

On 4 February 1596, James Burbage (like Peter Quince, a carpenter turned theatre impresario) had acquired a substantial property in Blackfriars and promptly converted it to a playhouse. Having made all his alterations, however, Burbage was prevented from actually using the new theatre following a petition to the Privy Council in November 1596 from neighbours complaining of the noise and other inconvenience that would be caused by the influx of playgoers, and the playhouse stood empty until 1600, when it was leased to a company of boy actors. Interestingly, one of the signatories to the 1596 petition was the company's own patron, George Carey, Lord Hunsdon, whose London home, Carey House, stood adjacent to the playhouse, and it has been argued that, if the play was designed for the wedding, Burbage's building, though not yet ready for performance, may have provided somewhere nearby for the company to prepare.

Wedding celebrations at this time often included performances, most commonly masque-like in nature (something of this kind is illustrated in the contemporary painting of the life and death of Sir Henry Unton that can be seen in the National Portrait Gallery in London), and usually mounted by friends and relatives rather than professional performers. However, in 1574 the Common Council of

London had specifically excluded from its responsibilities licensing 'plays, interludes, tragedies, comedies' performed to guests 'for the festivity of any marriage', and a year or two before *A Midsummer Night's Dream* was performed a group of players were paid £10 to perform at the wedding of the Earl of Northumberland. And, of course, though performed by an amateur group, *A Midsummer Night's Dream* itself includes a dramatic performance as a wedding entertainment.

David Wiles has been the strongest advocate of the play's original purpose being to celebrate an aristocratic wedding on 19 February 1596, when the new moon was conjunct with Pisces in Venus, which according to Elizabethan astrological interpretation was a particularly auspicious moment for weddings. This, he observes, would place the opening of the play some four days earlier (hence the stress on four days in the opening dialogue), on St Valentine's Day (14 February). When Theseus comes upon the lovers in the wood (IV.i.138–9), he comments that St Valentine's Day 'is past'. Wiles believes that because 'within the closed system of the text' Theseus' reference 'seems inconsequential' (1998, p. 68), the significance of the St Valentine's Day rituals in the play's structure have been overlooked, and he draws attention to the striking analogy between the game played on St Valentine's Day in which 'boy A chases girl B who chases boy C who chases girl D' and the plot structure of *A Midsummer Night's Dream* and to the custom whereby one's 'Valentine' is the first person one sees on waking (1998, p. 72). Wiles argues that Shakespeare has drawn together the rites of May and Valentine's days and merged them with the festival of Midsummer; together they 'reflect symbolically' the stages of 'mate selection, courtship and marriage' (1998, p. 77; also see Chapter 3, pp. 89–91).

Wiles's argument is thorough, but other critics (most comprehensively Gary Jay Williams, 1997, pp. 5–18) have strongly opposed this 'occasional performance' theory. They argue that it is based on no hard evidence, is counter to contemporary professional practices, and relies mainly on the play's culmination in three weddings and the reconciliation of the partners in an existing marriage, pointing out that many comedies end in weddings. Indeed, many critics observe that the play appears to problematise rather than celebrate both marriage and child–parent relationships by staging the conflicts inherent in them, so hardly making it a suitable wedding present either to give or to receive.

There can be no doubt, however, that, even if the play was first performed at Carey House, Shakespeare and his fellow members of the Lord Chamberlain's Men would from the outset have anticipated staging it publicly and commercially in the coming season in the summer of 1596, probably at the Theatre (an open air playhouse built by James Burbage and his brother-in-law, John Brayne in Shoreditch, in 1576). The Theatre stood a little west of where Shoreditch High Street is now, and was sited, like the other playhouses then operating (the Curtain – which stood near to the Theatre – the Rose and the recently opened Swan), just outside the city's boundaries and its jurisdiction. Although the excavations of the Rose playhouse in 1989 revealed considerable differences between that playhouse and what had been imagined as the generic shape and structure of Elizabethan open-air playhouses, it appears they shared a number of common features: a polygonal ground-plan, with tiered galleries for spectators (seated and possibly standing) surrounding a yard where audience members paid less to stand with no protection from the weather; a stage (which may have faced north at the Globe and definitely faced south at the Rose), probably around head-high and perhaps with a stage-trap, thrust out into the yard; a rear wall to the stage, with entrances on to the stage (two doors and, possibly, a larger central opening), behind which was the tiring house where the actors prepared themselves and waited for their cues. The stage of the Theatre was possibly (as stages were certainly in later playhouses) protected from the worst of the weather by a roof, supported by pillars, and perhaps had signs of the zodiac or other planetary images painted on its underside. The roof may also have contained some form of winching gear to lower a throne, for example, to the stage and (though more difficult) raise it up again. The printed text of *A Midsummer Night's Dream* suggests Shakespeare was thinking of such an outdoor physical structure rather than a hall in a private house: an entrance at the start of II.i refers to a Fairy entering at 'one door, and Robin Goodfellow at another door'; the central recess in the rear wall (if there was one; none is shown on the De Witt sketch of the Swan), covered with a hanging, might have been employed for Titania's bower (so removing the need for her actually to remain visible onstage between II.ii and III.i); while the frequent references to the moon might have involved acknowledgement of the decorated roof above the players' heads.

The play makes few technical demands. Its props list includes nothing that the company would not probably already possess or could not easily make. For example, the list of stage and other items listed in 1598 by Philip Henslowe, owner of the rival Rose playhouse, includes a lion skin and two lion heads, a cloth decorated with the sun and moon (possibly to be hung on the stage wall), two moss banks, and a robe 'for to go invisible'. These, or similar items, would be useful in a production of *A Midsummer Night's Dream* and presumably other companies possessed much the same kind of stock. The play's cast list, however, makes particular demands on the company's acting resources. As a general rule, plays performed by Shakespeare's company require around 12 adult actors with, in addition, no more than four youths to play the female roles which, in the case of *A Midsummer Night's Dream*, would account for Hippolyta, Titania, Hermia and Helena. However, while we know that companies regularly assigned two or more parts to an actor, in only a few instances do the surviving character lists indicate how the doubling was to be organised. It has become common in modern productions to double the roles of Theseus and Oberon, and Hippolyta and Titania, but there is no evidence for this practice, thematically or practically, within the text itself (though see the Commentary for IV.i.102–10). A number of critics have assumed that the fairies in the play were intended by Shakespeare to be played by youths (Bloom, 1999, p. 163, even asserts they were performed by children, as indeed they often have been, but there's no evidence for this), and have used this as further support for the play's having been originally conceived for a private occasion, where the company's usual complement of performers could be supplemented, perhaps by child (as opposed to youthful) actors. However, contemporary views on fairies indicate that they were thought to be of human size, and the play's clear statements that they had sexual relationships with adult humans suggest that Shakespeare imagined the parts to be played by adult actors, relying as usual on his words and the audience's imaginations to create the sense where necessary of the fairies' diminutive stature.

For the most part, we can at best only speculate about how the play was originally staged. Ronald Watkins and Jeremy Lemmon (*In Shakespeare's Playhouse: A Midsummer Night's Dream*, 1974) bravely make a number of confident assumptions – that at the start of Act I scene ii, for example, the 'Chamber-curtains open to reveal the familiar members of the company's comedy gang' (p. 45) or as the following scene begins the First Fairy 'comes from one of the main Doors and busily attaches a leafy bough to a Stage-Post, converting it immediately into a tree' (p. 53). I am not saying their guesses are wrong, but they *are* guesses (and based on a model of the playhouse that has, inevitably, been revised since they wrote). Similarly, C. Walter Hodges has produced sketches of how Titania's bower might have been staged (reproduced in Foakes 2003, p. 34), but these involve the use of an 'inner stage' which is challenged by other theatre historians.

However, what we know of the open-air playhouse does fit securely with the fundamental needs of the staging indicated by the text. If there was a larger central entrance (such as there was at the Globe) it would have presumably been used for the imposing procession that opens the play, while the doors each side of the rear wall (specifically referred to in the stage direction at the start of II.i) would have been effective in bringing opposed forces face to face, such as the entry of Titania and Oberon at line 59 in that scene. Until their arrival, there are only two characters on stage. This rises to at least ten (assuming three fairy attendants for each monarch) until line 145 when only Puck and Oberon remain. From line 176, Oberon is alone on stage for 12 lines before the arrival of Demetrius and Helena, before Oberon is left alone briefly for two lines and the scene ends, as it began, with two spirits on stage. Interestingly, as this scene indicates, and experiences on the stage at the Globe reconstruction have confirmed, the large platform stage accommodates large and small, formal and intimate groupings of actors, and 'naturalness' works as well as spectacle.

At III.ii.357, Oberon instructs Puck to create a fog 'as black as Acheron' to confuse Lysander and Demetrius. Although we know that smoke was used (if rarely) to create effects on the Elizabethan stage, it seems more likely that mists or fogs on stage were fictional, created by the actors' behaviour. The posts that supported the roof above the stage might also have been directly employed in the staging: they were used to represent trees to sit under, pin things to, or climb, and so might have represented the Duke's oak beneath which the Mechanicals meet to rehearse (White 1998, pp. 120–3). There was also a balcony at the rear of the stage, which could be used as part of the action (as in *Romeo and Juliet*) or, more often, for one or more characters to observe the onstage action.

Elizabethan playing companies laid out considerable sums of money on costuming their productions when something more than conventional dress was required. In *The Merry Wives of Windsor* it appears the fairies were dressed in usual male or female clothes in green and white, with their faces (or masks) painted black, grey, green or white. Although intended for performances of masques at court, Inigo Jones' designs for costumes for an unspecified winged figure and for a fiery spirit (in *The Lord's Masque*, 1612), and for an armoured Oberon, without wings (in his 1611 masque of that name), may suggest how these figures were presented on stage. The mortals probably wore costumes reflecting a mix of Greco-Roman and romance elements, with the mechanicals dressed as Elizabethan artisans.

In *A Midsummer Night's Dream*, perhaps more than any other of his plays, Shakespeare explores the specific relationship between image and imagination, language and object, illusion and reality. Awareness of the play's possible first conditions of performance may explain why later performances that engage the imagination through the ear rather than, or at least more than, the eye can seem to touch more acutely the heart of the play.

2   Commentary

Reading an old play, especially one as well known as this, and trying to do so as if, in Trevor Nunn's phrase, it has just come through the letterbox, is not easy. Nor is it that straightforward to put to the back of one's mind the books and critical essays one has read, or the performances one has seen or – even harder – been part of. But while study and performance can be of considerable help in broadening our understanding of the text or seeing alternative ways of doing things, both are also likely to narrow our initial response to the play. In other words, it is important, first of all, to try to explore every little corner of the text, always bearing in mind that it will be full of signals to the actors that will help them shape the performance. At the same time (the lovers' quarrel in the wood is a good example, the mechanicals' play a better one) each performance will find small details of physical action and 'business' that arise from the particular circumstances of the director's ideas or the actors' inventiveness in rehearsal and there is no point in my trying to forecast or prescribe (or indeed, proscribe) these.

In rehearsal, however well some of those involved might know the text, it is crucial to act (at least at first) only what is happening at that precise moment. What has gone before may, of course, shape the action – but not what is to come. I have tried (though not dogmatically) to follow this principle in the Commentary, to avoid what one might call, in rehearsal terms, playing the whole play at once. Of course, once one gets to the end of a scene, or the whole play, one can look back at those earlier signals – which may not always be apparent at the time – that prefigure what is to come and, where necessary, adjust. On some occasions, however, where a word or an idea emerges that has a bearing on the tone of the play overall, I have commented, rather as one might intervene in the read-through of a play, and these comments are printed in italics. Of course, the great thing about plays – even more so in Shakespeare's theatre than our own where, outdoors at least, they had no intervals – is that they keep moving. There is no opportunity to rewind to catch something we missed or to fast-forward through bits we may find boring or to ponder the possible meanings of a line or action with the help of a footnote. But I have introduced at some points a brief reflection on what's happened, how we have moved on, how our understanding and expectations may have changed. I have not imagined the play on any stage in particular, but have often related the text to the characteristics of Shakespeare's playhouse to underline the fundamental interaction of verbal and physical stage languages: it is up to any modern performance to translate those into its own terms.

Act I

Act I, scene i

o *Enter* Theseus, Hippolyta, *with others*. Watching a modern performance, assisted by a programme that lists the characters 'in order of speaking' or 'of appearance' we will know that Theseus is the Duke of Athens and Hippolyta is the Queen of the Amazons. Who the 'others' are, the early texts do not make clear, but they obviously include Philostrate (who has no other entrance marked and is addressed by Theseus at line 11) and, presumably, the attendants of the Duke and Queen. The scene is set somewhere in Theseus' court in Athens, though a performance will need to decide where the characters are entering from, the specific place they are coming into, and the reason why they come here. The staging of these opening moments of the play have included impressive processions (particularly popular in the nineteenth century), the return from a hunting trip, or an intimate private conversation between the two characters.

1–6 Theseus' reference to the four days they must wait before the wedding takes place raises the question 'why must they?' He's evidently in charge, so we might presume he sets the rules. Maybe it's just because that's the date that has been set for what is undoubtedly a major event. But his specific reference to the period until this moon wanes and 'another moon' emerges indicates that the scene is set during the darkest part of the moon's cycle, a time believed by the Elizabethans to be inauspicious for marriages. Furthermore, it was a time associated with a woman's menstrual period, during which sexual activity was associated with the likelihood of producing a malformed baby – what the Elizabethans termed a 'moon-calf' – an outcome that Theseus, slayer of the Minotaur, a bull-headed man – might be especially anxious to avoid (Penguin edition, 2005, pp. xxv–xxvi). When the character names his bride-to-be as Hippolyta, for many in Shakespeare's audience (though a modern one will probably need that programme), he is immediately identified as Theseus, King (or in this case, Duke), of Athens – a city famed as the traditional home of reason. However, the mood of Theseus' opening speech might seem to us more melancholic than festive: it is rather like the opening lines of *Twelfth Night* in that respect. The blank verse lines have the flexibility of prose, running seamlessly into each other, while it is the *sound* and *rhythm* of the language, as much as the meaning of the words themselves, that affects us. For example, the repeated 'o' sounds, and the phrase 'linger my desires' (which resists being spoken quickly), embody Theseus' sense of frustration at the slowness with which time is passing before his wedding and the urgency of his wish to satisfy his desires. Indeed, Theseus' impatience draws from him an image that might strike us as less than romantic, even curiously negative, as he casts the moon as a wealthy old woman 'Long *withering* out a young man's revenue' (again the verb slows the speaker down) by refusing to die.

7–11 By contrast, Hippolyta's lines – made up predominantly of monosyllables with short vowels – are brisker, more matter-of-fact, suggesting that the time will pass 'quickly', which she emphasises by repeating the word. Her response might be seen as balancing his, reassuring him, suggesting she accepts the situation and is even happy to wait for the time to pass. But her words might equally hint at a difference in their perspective on the forthcoming marriage: that what he can't wait for is approaching all too quickly for her. Hippolyta also restores a more lyrical image of the moon, and one entirely appropriate for a warrior Queen. Editors now generally print 'New bent' in line 10, but the early editions' 'Now bent' seems to me preferable: it perfectly describes the thin crescent of a waning moon, and the image is further enforced if Hippolyta carries her bow, emblematic of her warrior status and with its echoes of Diana, the moon-goddess and huntress. Moreover, 'Now bent' also catches the sense of tension waiting to be released that underpins these exchanges. Her final word 'solemnity' has been interpreted as sounding a sombre note, but it was also commonly used at the time to describe a mood of celebration. Of course, there's no reason why it should not carry something of both meanings – what Peter Brook calls a 'vibrating' word – and so alert us (as with Theseus' 'dowager' image, and the tone of these opening lines overall) to the range of emotions eddying around these characters' relationship to each other and their situation.

These opening speeches have laid great stress on the moon, an image that will pervade and unify the play across its groupings of characters and plot lines before appearing personified in the play of Pyramus and Thisbe. The moon oversees the night, a time we associate with romance and sexual activity, it is commonly associated with madness, and is an emblem of change. 'Midsummer Night' is 23 June. Later in the play we will hear Theseus refer to the lovers rising early to observe the 'rite of May' (IV.i.132). In fact, the Elizabethan customs surrounding Maying were not confined to May Day (1 May), but were spread across the summer months and Shakespeare seems more interested in the general sense of courtship rituals. Later, we may notice, too, that the action of the play has taken place over two days and a single night. At this point, however, Theseus' reference to 'four days' is presumably to underscore the sense of frustration he expresses, but Hippolyta's reference to the fact that they – and we – will quickly 'dream away' the time, is perhaps more important in signalling the particular state of mind the play will explore in which dream logic will take precedence over reality (Garber 1974, chapter 2, passim and Further Reading.) In Elizabethan court poetry Queen Elizabeth was frequently associated with the moon (as Diana or Cynthia, for example), the analogy often enforcing the Queen's very public status as a virgin. But as has often been observed, the somewhat negative image of the moon employed here, and the association of virginity with 'the cold fruitless moon' later in this scene (I.i.73), are set against the examples of sexual love and fertility that triumph at the close of the play. This apparent contradiction is possible because the image of the moon was, like so many contemporary emblems, multi-faceted – on the one hand signifying divine virginity (as with Diana) and, on the other, implying withdrawal from the world, even irrationality. Consequently, in the complex, often coded modes of writing common to the Elizabethans, poets and playwrights could appear to praise and celebrate the queen while an audience willing to decipher another meaning might see one that alluded more critically to the declining power of the ageing monarch.

11–15   Seemingly encouraged by Hippolyta's words (line 11 is significantly shared between them, invariably a clue to the actors of some
specific contact – emotional, intellectual, physical, etc – between
speakers), Theseus instructs Philostrate (pronounced with a long 'a'
and an accented final 'e', rather than to rhyme with 'great') to arrange
some entertainment that will banish the pervading melancholic
mood, which he personifies, as he did with the 'withering' dowager
image, as a 'pale companion'. Philostrate obeys without replying,
but we can deduce from the task he is given that he acts as Theseus'
Master of the Revels, responsible (as Elizabeth's own Master, Henry
Tilney, was) for providing performances and other entertainments
at court.

16–19   Theseus' lines reveal to us the 'back story' of his relationship with Hippolyta, and the violence that has led to this match;
he wooed Hippolyta with his sword (commonly associated with
'penis' in Elizabethan literature), 'doing [her] injuries' However, he
promises to wed her 'in another key', an indication of a change in
manner and tone that we will need to keep track of. As her dress
and bearing will testify, Hippolyta is an Amazon, queen of a tribe of
warrior women who reputedly removed their right breasts to make
it easier to shoot a bow (see p. 97). Theseus' speech might start to
offer an explanation of the cause of the nervousness between the
characters, a tension that (depending on how the scene has been
played) might have been felt so far even by a modern audience, who
unlike many in the original playhouse, will not bring with them a
ready-formed knowledge of Theseus. For as well as being famed as
a man of reason and a warrior who slew the half-man, half-beast,
the Cretan Minotaur, conquered the Amazons and carried off
their queen (also, confusingly, called Antiope) with whom he had
a son, the ill-fated Hippolytus, Theseus was also the first seducer
of Helen, a serial womaniser and betrayer of his lovers. The Roman
author Plutarch, from whom Shakespeare took some details of this
couple (see pp. 96–7), points out that Theseus' interest in women
was for his own gratification and 'was rather to satisfy lust than
of any great love' for the women involved. A 'triumph' (line 19)
was specifically a procession awarded to one victorious in battle.
Until the 1960s, Theseus and Hippolyta were generally presented
on stage as already being reconciled by the start of the play, before

performances began to see their relationship as initially fractious. A production of the play by John Hancock for the Actors' Workshop, San Francisco, in 1966, emphasized Hippolyta's status as one of the spoils of war: played by a black actress, she was brought on stage in a cage made of black bamboo, dressed in a tiger skin and speaking her 'romantic' lines with a snarling sarcasm. In Karin Beier's 1995 production (see p. 117) she was brought on naked and then dressed in Western clothes by Theseus' attendants as an emblematic act of forced assimilation. More recently, Greg Doran's 2005/8 RSC production opened with a mimed duel between Theseus and Hippolyta that established before a word was spoken the combative nature of their 'courtship'.

Enter Egeus *and his daughter* Hermia, *and* Lysander *and* Demetrius

20–5   The tone of seriousness in the opening of the scene, the tension between the need to restrain passion and the imminent prospect of release, is now complicated by the arrival of Egeus 'full of vexation', with his daughter Hermia (who, we learn later from the text, but will usually immediately see on stage, is short and dark) and two young men, Lysander and Demetrius. All these new characters are named almost immediately (and now Theseus is named for the first time too, for anyone who hasn't worked out who or what he is). The early editions indicate that Helena should also enter at this point, but the character does not speak until line 181, which is where modern editors and performances commonly place her entrance. It is worth considering, however, what effect her silent presence might have in the scene; it would certainly be worth exploring in rehearsal.

26–45   Egeus' instructions, first to Demetrius, then to Lysander, to 'stand forth' were originally printed as stage directions. Although the fact that the lines are regular iambic pentameters might suggest they should be (as they invariably are by editors) attributed to Egeus, their original nature suggests some formality in the staging of the confrontation as the scene from this point takes on the nature of a trial (a scene popular in early modern plays). It has even been suggested that the original audience might have recognised here the stock characters and pattern of Roman New Comedy, and, momentarily at least, have thought that this is itself a performance, perhaps brought in response to Theseus' command for entertainment (Belsey 1993, p. 188). It is a view encouraged by the behaviour and words of this angry father (the *senex iratus* of classical comedy) who claims the rituals of youthful courtship are nothing less than witchcraft, and who sees the young lover, Lysander, as no more than a common thief who has 'filched' (meaning to steal in an underhand way) his property. It is a concrete and detailed attack from Egeus, but one that will almost certainly have the effect of swinging our support behind Hermia and her desire to marry the man she loves. And if any of what Egeus says about Lysander is true, it will start to give us an impression of this young man as someone who apparently spends his time writing love poems, singing softly (the meaning of the first 'feigning' in line 31) and inundating an impressionable young woman with love tokens: a production in Maine in 1982, for example, presented Lysander as a young Tennyson, jotting down verses.

Egeus' querulous tone and the excessiveness of his language may render him comic at first, and that's one way he can be, and often is, played. But an actor performs a role from the *character's* point of view, and Egeus undoubtedly believes he is in the right, and is supported by the 'ancient privilege of Athens' in his demand not just that Hermia should marry a man of *his* choosing (a view with which most Elizabethan fathers would probably have agreed) but that if she refuses – we will be shocked to hear – she should be condemned to death according to the law.

46–51 Perhaps again to our surprise, Theseus endorses Egeus' views, and picking up on Egeus' description of Hermia as 'unhardened' (meaning 'impressionable', line 35), confirms that a daughter should be moulded as wax only by her all-powerful father into whatever form *he* wishes: indeed, Theseus' phrase that Egeus may 'figure, or disfigure' (mar) her, is itself a particularly threatening one.

52–7 The two suitors are hardly distinguishable, except for the fact that Demetrius is the preferred choice of Hermia's father, while Hermia has chosen Lysander. Indeed, it's never really clear why Egeus prefers one to the other; it may be he is simply more interested in being obeyed. Which young man is the better choice is a question of individual perception and Hermia now addresses what was a key concern of the time and a frequent topic in plays: the relation between seeing and judging, between the desire she and Lysander feel for each other (which is powerful but can be wayward and often misguided), and reason (here represented by Theseus/Egeus) that seeks to control those desires and try to ensure judgement prevails.

58–64 If Egeus is one of Shakespeare's possessive and controlling fathers (others include Capulet, Shylock, Brabantio, Prospero and Lear) Hermia is emerging as one of Shakespeare's unruly daughters, such as Katherine (*The Taming of the Shrew*), Juliet, Jessica (*The Merchant of* Venice), Desdemona and Rosalind, each of whom challenges her father's assumed right to decide the course of her life. Now, as if Hermia recognises the implacable stance taken by her father and Theseus, and as if her love has armed her with the strength to mount a defence, she calmly and politely asks what – if she persists in making her own choice – will be her fate.

65–6 Theseus' answer, confirming the law, comes with no hesitation. It is a key moment, and recognising its impact on those present, Granville Barker instructed his cast to 'all play to this'. At this point the play almost holds its breath: it teeters on the edge of taking either a comic or tragic path, and as an audience (if the play were new to us) we might be more likely to assume it will follow the latter.

67–90 But immediately Theseus provides a glimmer of hope by offering Hermia the choice to enter a monastery rather than be executed. As if guiding her in making a decision, Theseus sets his references to sexual desire, marriage and generation against an image of virginity as a secluded, constrained, single and barren life, with the moon here identified with Diana, goddess of chastity. He acknowledges the strength of those who subdue their sexual passion to live a chaste life, but argues (drawing on the image of the rose, a symbol of virginity, and repeating his earlier word 'withering') that it is those who marry who gain greater happiness in life. But, again, Hermia stands up for her right to choose her own husband, daring to suggest that she has a claim to the property in herself ('virgin patent' is again a legalistic phrase). Theseus, aware of the serious implications of her answer, gives her the time remaining before his own wedding day to make up her mind. His phrase, 'sealing day', with its resonance both of a wedding contract and death, sustains the frame-work of contrasts on which the scene on every level has worked so far. The narrative drive towards a culmination of these two incom-patible events – a wedding and execution – is now focused on the same end point, a few days away.

91–110   It may be the measured, reasonable tone with which these dangerous matters are being discussed that prompts the outbursts from Demetrius (using the same legal terms of possession that tie him to Egeus) and Lysander. Lysander's startlingly impertinent line will undoubtedly raise a laugh from the audience – the first in the play so far, perhaps – and suddenly releases the valve on this pres-sured scene. It certainly reinforces Egeus' own view of this youth's unsuitability, and he again asserts his right to 'estate' (another legal term meaning to bestow) his daughter to whom he wishes. George Bernard Shaw thought Lysander's lines (99 on) should be spoken pri-vately to Theseus, but they are surely a public statement, pointing out to all present – including Egeus – how little there is to choose between him and Demetrius in terms of status and wealth. Of course, the actors chosen to play the roles will bring an individual physique, voice and manner to each part, and our first impressions from the text will probably suggest Demetrius as something of an Egeus in the making, while Lysander, who spends his time bombard-ing Hermia with love-tokens and writing love poetry, appears more romantic. But Lysander has something of a bombshell to lob into the scene, something that surely takes the wind out of Demetrius' sails and is likely to draw to him the beady eye of Hermia's father. According to Lysander, Helena 'dotes, / Devoutly dotes, dotes in idol-atry' upon Demetrius. (In fact, 'dote', which suggests disproportion-ate affection, is used eight times in the play, more than in any other work by Shakespeare, including the sonnets.)

111–21   A performance will need to decide who on stage – apart from Lysander and Demetrius – knows about this alleged affair with Helena. Maybe Demetrius will want to deny it, but he has no chance to do so before Theseus confirms that he has also heard about it (does Egeus wonder why no one told *him*?) and rather quickly tries to pass on by preparing to exit. The fact that Theseus knows something of these young people's affairs, and the ease with which they all speak in his presence, indicates that they are not far removed in social standing from the Duke. I am not sure exactly what the 'private schooling' is that Theseus has planned for Egeus and Demetrius, or if it is the same as the 'business' concerning his wedding. Perhaps, by taking everyone with him, he simply wants to give Lysander and Hermia an opportunity to be alone. Maybe – as a man himself impatient to seal an 'everlasting bond of fellowship' in marriage (line 85) – he wants to try to talk father and would-be suitor out of pursuing this clearly loveless match and to let Hermia make her own choice. But his departing line to Hermia, with its forceful alliteration in line 118, will leave her in little doubt of the serious decision she has to make.

122–7 We may have noticed in reading, but will certainly notice in performance, that Hippolyta, though on stage throughout, has not spoken since line 11, and apart from the moment when Theseus' reference to his imminent marriage presumably includes acknowledgement of her, she has not been the focus of attention. However, *how* she responds throughout the scene to what she sees and hears is significant, especially if in Hermia's situation she sees something of her own 'captive' state. Or does she respond more to the fact that she has been more or less totally ignored by everyone, underlining, perhaps, her 'difference' from the Athenians? Theseus' 'what cheer' (line 122) might mean 'cheer up' ('cheer' could refer to a facial expression) or he might be asking her what she would like in the way of entertainment, but his question is undoubtedly prompted by her evident mood (though has he registered *why* she looks upset?). Whichever they decide, these are key questions for the actors.

128–55 The departure of Theseus, Hippolyta, Egeus, Demetrius and the attendants leaves Hermia and Lysander alone (not a situation either Egeus or Demetrius probably likes much). The situation and the mood are grave, and there can as yet be no certainty that it will resolve itself happily, and so Lysander's first lines to Hermia might appear to be rather ill judged, especially as her resolute demeanour before Theseus has now given way to floods of tears. Of course, he might play the lines as a deliberate joke to cheer her up, but they might equally suggest he has not entirely grasped what's going on. Or maybe he's experiencing the difficulty most of us have in finding the right words when faced with another person's distress. But Hermia's response takes him at face value, and the tone and language of the scene shift. It is not uncommon for critics and performers to look for musical analogies when discussing the patterned forms of Shakespeare's language, and here it is as if the characters have broken into a duet. At a not dissimilar moment in *Romeo and Juliet* (I.v) the lovers spin a sonnet together, and the effect in both instances is the same: here, the alternate lines (*stichomythia*) convey a sense of the rapport and intimacy between them (Shaw thought their words set 'the whole scene throbbing with their absorption in one another') as she interrupts the flow of his argument, while, at the same time, the formal, conventional nature of the language serves to extend their individual experience so that it acquires a more general application – the 'customary cross' born by all lovers, as Hermia describes it (line 153). In such instances, the actors have two particular tasks common to all performers in complex language plays such as this: to make the formal language sound as it is the only language they can speak while not losing sight of its patterned and heightened nature (what the director, Adrian Noble, calls 'cracking the form'). In Peter Thomson's fine phrase, Shakespeare had learned he could 'play the solo instruments of the lyric against the groundswell of the narrative' (1999, p. 108), without losing the attention of his audience.

156–79 To avoid the threat to Hermia, Lysander introduces a plan that drives the plot in a new direction, and beyond the confines of city and palace. Picking up on Theseus' earlier 'stepdame' image (line 5), Lysander makes the rich widow real: she is now his aunt, he the child she never had. Her home, deep in the forest will not only be a place beyond the reach of the 'sharp Athenian law' but also, interestingly, a place where he and Hermia can be safely married, either by entering into a contract to marry in the future, which was binding but not sanctified by a priest, or maybe there's a friendly friar he knows who can perform the ceremony. Picking up on his line (line 168), and perhaps at this point embracing him (the first physical contact we've seen between any of the characters, I imagine), Hermia pledges herself to Lysander, drawing on examples and legends from classical mythology to enforce the strength of her commitment, and gently slipping into the rhyming couplets in which (apart from line 179) the rest of the scene is written. This gives her words a particular quality (almost as if anticipating her marriage vows) while still sustaining the present tense of the moment by her playful joke comparing male and female fidelity, which no doubt prompts a gentle protest from Lysander.

Enter Helena

179–80 We have heard about, but not met, Helena before, and Lysander immediately introduces her for us. Given her role in the conflict between the other three young people she is instantly of interest. Lysander's lines suggest Helena has not come to look for them, but is either passing on her way somewhere else or, coming across the lovers in an obviously intimate and private moment (perhaps they're kissing), is trying to reverse out again before they see her.

181–225 Helena rhymes her first line with Hermia's, a verbal emblem of their closeness, and continues to speak in rhyme. Her comparison of Hermia's eyes to 'lodestars' (which guide travellers), and her voice to the song of the lark in spring and early summer 'when wheat is green and hawthorn buds appear' – an image drawn from Shakespeare's own observation in the Warwickshire fields, no doubt – allows the playwright to express not only Helena's sense of seeing her lover (Demetrius) lured away by her best friend's charms, but also, in its detail, to evoke the world of the countryside as a real place in their lives. Helena's words tumble out of her as she expresses her wish to be more like Hermia: indeed, she wants to be 'translated' – or transformed – into Hermia (though we won't register the particular significance of this verb at this point). Physically different these young women may be (and as readers we need to keep this in our minds at all times), but Shakespeare has chosen to give them slightly similar names. Why? Because, I think, he wants to underline that they, like the two young men, though to a lesser degree, are to some extent interchangeable. However, while we are never certain of the relationship between the two men (though the actors may choose to make this up for themselves), we learn from Hermia that she and Helena have long been intimate friends, on many occasions wandering into the wood to pour out their hearts and secrets to each other. At line 194 they move into stichomythia, a verbal rally (though here it is a debate rather than the earlier love-duet) in which – as he often

does in his early plays – Shakespeare rather ostentatiously displays
a range of rhetorical techniques: repeating words or phrases at the
beginning of successive clauses (technically known as *anaphora*),
creating phrases of equal length (*isocolon*), and balancing gram-
matical parts of a sentence (*parison*). This is a deliberate demonstra-
tion of the writer's mastery of this aspect of his craft, but we need,
more importantly, to understand the *dramatic* purposes and *theatrical*
effects of such linguistic strategies, which here are used to underline
the tension between formality of language and the complexity of the
relationships. For example, if the edition you are using has printed
'sweet' at the end of line 216, and 'stranger companies' at the end of
line 219 (as the New Cambridge and Penguin editions do, for example), I suggest you consider restoring the early editions' 'swelled' and
'strange companions'. Editors usually make the changes to continue
the rhyming couplets, but (remembering that he is a better writer
than his editors) Shakespeare might well be intentionally disrupt-
ing the rhyme scheme and the sense of harmony its regularity would
otherwise suggest. The exchange is brought to an end by Hermia's
firm assertion (enforced by placing her friend's name in line 200) that
the problem lies with Demetrius' desires, not her own, and she reas-
sures Helena that she, Hermia, will soon be out of the picture. But
strangely, while she and Lysander tell of their plans to flee, lyrically
evoking the night and the woods as a romantic place of refuge, they
omit to tell Helena of the pressing danger that makes their departure
necessary. (Of course, if Helena does enter scene one when the quarto
stage direction suggests she does, she would already know.)

226–end of scene   Helena is left alone, the first time a solitary
character has occupied the stage. Conventionally (at least in modern
performance practice and, I believe, in the early modern playhouse,
too), a soliloquy is an opportunity for a character to engage directly
and honestly with an audience, a rapport sometimes compromised
when Shakespeare's plays are performed on stages that don't share the
same actor/audience relationship as the playhouses he wrote for. Here,
Helena works through her dilemma with us. Rhyming couplets by their
very nature might suggest that a character's ideas are fully formed. But
equally, the *finding* of a rhyme can suggest the character coming to a
realisation, or a discovery, such as, perhaps, when it dawns on Helena
why Cupid is 'painted blind', with the repetition of 'therefore' further

indicating her journey of ideas. The form also allows her to move from the general – repeating the point Hermia made earlier about the balance in love between sight and judgement – to focus on her own situation. Her annoyance with Demetrius (and the difficulty she evidently has in entirely absolving Hermia from any responsibility) is brilliantly caught in the alliterative 'h' in lines 243–4: words beginning with 'h' demand a particular energy from the speaker and a strong exhalation of breath. It is also another example of Shakespeare's wordplay, with a complex pun on 'hail': the first use of 'hail' as a verb means to 'pour down with great force', but it also *sounds* like 'hale', to 'pull down' as if from the sky, while the second 'hail' is a noun, and likens Demetrius' oaths to hailstones, easily melted in the heat of Hermia's attentions. Helena does not heed her own argument, however, and her decision to betray Hermia and Lysander's plan to Demetrius reveals that, indeed, 'love's mind' has not 'of any judgement taste'.

This opening scene has covered a great deal of ground. It has laid the foundations for what appears at this point to be going to be a play of conflicts between youth and age, and between men and women. It has introduced us to two sets of lovers, the mature aristocratic couple, and the young courtiers, and the complication presented by parental opposition. It has also alerted us to the range, variety and flexibility of the stage languages, verbal and physical, that Shakespeare employs. Granville Barker noted that Shakespeare liked his plays to have a good firm jumping off point and the opening scene has provided just that. But with its competing mix of comic and serious tones we cannot be certain in which direction – towards a tragic or comic conclusion – the play is headed. Indeed, whether this play or Romeo and Juliet was written first, the plays' evident relationships at the levels of character, plot and tone remind us of Shakespeare's – and Elizabethan and Jacobean drama in general's – constant desire to mingle contrasting moods as an expression of the writers' awareness that human experience is always a mixture of emotional experiences.

Act I, scene ii

0 *Enter* Quince *the Carpenter, and* Snug *the Joiner, and* Bottom *the Weaver, and* Flute *the Bellows-mender, and* Snout *the Tinker and* Starveling *the Tailor.* From Theseus' palace, the scene moves to Quince's workshop, somewhere in the 'city' (line 95) of Athens (though Shakespeare's reference to it also as a 'town' at line 94 may suggest he had somewhere more like Stratford-upon-Avon in mind). After scene one, and even before we learn their names, the different position of these men in the social hierarchy of the play's world will be apparent from their clothes and accents, while their occupations will be evident to us from the various tools of their trades.

1–12   It quickly becomes apparent that these working men are – or have formed themselves into – a 'company' of amateur actors, who are gathered to rehearse a play in response to Theseus' call in the opening scene for revels to celebrate his marriage. (No record of such a group exists from Shakespeare's time; Dobson 2003.) Competitiveness and uncertainty are in the air, as they often are on the first day of rehearsals. Peter Quince, the director (and author) of their 'interlude' (a short dramatic piece designed to be performed between parts of a larger event or entertainment) speaks first, holding the yet-to-be-revealed cast list close to his chest. Although he clearly includes all present in his opening remarks, it is one of the actors, Bottom, who appoints himself as the sole respondent, and who wants to drive things along. The proposed play – a 'lamentable comedy' that treats merrily of a 'cruel death' –parodies the titles of near-contemporary plays, and may signal the confusion that surrounds their artistic endeavour, but it also echoes the mix of moods we have just encountered in the opening scene. We will notice if reading, and should hear in performance, the shift from the verse of the preceding scene to the prose of this. Verse is the dominant form of Shakespeare's early comedies (around 70% in each) and so the change will certainly be evident. But the scene is in prose not only to signal the change in status of the characters and location of the scene (Prince Hamlet speaks a good deal of prose in royal Elsinore) but also to reflect the 'grounded' nature of these artisans.

13–37   Bottom's 'spread yourselves' suggests the actors have been clustered around Quince, perhaps trying to get a look at the cast list and learn what part they've been given.

A quince is a fruit whose name derives from the fourteenth century 'quoyn', which in turn suggests 'quoins', usually interpreted as the wedges used by carpenters and printers to secure items. But 'quoins' refers also (and more commonly) to dressed stones at the corners of buildings, stones that, interestingly, are said to be 'squint' when they are not set at right angles. That might be a useful link to the character's name and, for the actor, alongside ideas around the sour taste and yellow appearance of a quince, offer possibilities for his appearance, vocal tone and physical manner. (Perhaps of less direct use to an actor, but interesting nevertheless, is that in Spanish the word for 'quince' is 'membrillo', or 'little member' (or penis) and that as well as being a well-known aphrodisiac it was associated in Shakespeare's time with weddings in Athens; see Parker 2003.)

Casting begins. Nick Bottom the weaver is first.

A 'bottom' is an implement used in weaving to wind thread, or the ball of thread itself, but did Shakespeare also think it would be comic for someone to be called Bottom? He chose to call a character in Measure for Measure 'Pompey Bum' (who is nicknamed 'Pompey the Great' by other characters because 'your bum is the greatest thing about you' II.i.214–5). The OED's earliest use of 'bottom' to mean 'buttocks' is dated 1794, but Dekker calls a character in The Shoemaker's Holiday (1600) 'Mistress Frigbottom' which might suggest that something of the later sense already existed, and Elizabethan writers often punned on ass/arse (Patterson 1989). Bottom is often played as a rather portly, middle-aged man, but there is no basis whatsoever in the text for this, unless we read Quince's description of Pyramus as a 'sweet youth and tall' as a piece of comic irony. Hazlitt (1817) called him 'the most romantic of mechanics', and the frontispiece to Bell's 1774 edition and a number of paintings have portrayed a Bottom more in line with Glynne Wickham's description of him as 'a good looking young workman' with a striking physique (1969, p. 187). Michael Hoffman's film, by casting Kevin Kline in the role, took a similar view (see Chapter 5).

Bottom is certainly not short on confidence, speaking eight lines of a play from memory (giving him an opportunity to try to move his audience with the passion of his performance and Shakespeare to poke fun at outdated styles of writing and performing), praising his own performance ('This was lofty'), underlining how he will modify the 'tyrant's vein' (his 'chief humour') to suit a lover, noting that tears might be needed (often, then and now, considered by audiences a sign of 'real' acting) and looking out for what else he might do in the play. But it is important that the actor plays Bottom seriously, truthfully: 'he must be very good at what he does, even when he's ridiculous – especially when he's ridiculous' (Abraham 2005, p. 21). At the same time, Bottom is undeniably rather pompous, frequently affecting words of some scale, for instance, but invariably pronouncing them wrongly.

38–50   Flute, the bellows-mender, is chosen to play the female role of Thisbe, presumably because he has a lighter voice, one that resembles the whistle of air as a bellows is blown to boost a fire, or the reedy noise of a small organ, powered by bellows (sometimes used in indoor playhouses) and so more suited to a female role. Disappointed that he's not to play a heroic male role (and seemingly sensitive to the implicit comment on his masculinity), Flute's protestations are no doubt increased by the ribbing he gets from the others: an actor can pretty much guarantee a laugh if he pauses after referring to his (clearly barely visible) 'beard', and uses 'coming' to quell the teasing of his fellows. But Bottom is on hand to claim the role of Thisbe, too, and demonstrates how he would play it. Bottom's affectation of 'Thisne' (spoken in his 'condoling' voice) is a bit puzzling; maybe it's an attempt to suggest Pyramus' pet name for his lover, before he adopts a higher pitched voice as Flute. Whichever it is, Quince is having none of it, and calls the company to order.

51–61   Quince, realising that Bottom will offer himself in all the roles, moves swiftly to wind things up and fit each part to an actor: Robin Starveling – evidently intended to look as thin and weak as tailors proverbially were, and a role possibly originally played by the famously thin actor, John Sincler – is to play Thisbe's mother, Snout (a tinker, used to mending spouts) is cast as Pyramus' father, while Quince will play Thisbe's father and Snug, the joiner (who makes snug fitting joints), is to play the lion.

62–end of scene   Quince's efforts to complete casting and move on are thwarted by Snug (memorably described by one nineteenth century critic as a man 'who can board and lodge only one idea at a time and that tardily'), who reveals that he is 'slow of study'. Snug's confession immediately prompts Bottom to offer to take on that part as well. Bottom must roar well, but his malapropism-filled effort to counter Quince's diversionary tactic that he would be too convincing in the role – by offering to 'aggravate' his voice and roar like a nightingale – draws an unexpected firmness from the director: 'You can play no part but Pyramus'. This is, however, followed immediately by a good deal of flattery, and the punctuation of Quince's lines (79–82) in the first quarto indicates a pause after each phrase, as he works to placate his star performer, who is now presumably in a huff of rejection and must be soothed. That achieved, however, no one, least of all Quince, is much interested in Bottom's quandary about which colour beard he will use, though it draws from Quince a mildly vulgar joke about the baldness caused by venereal disease – a joke a modern audience will be hard pressed to spot, let alone find funny. As he distributes the parts, Quince instructs his cast to meet in a secluded spot in the wood, that night, where they may rehearse undisturbed. There's a good visual theatrical joke in the distribution of parts. In the early modern theatre (and indeed, up to the 1930s) actors received only their own 'part' – a sheet with just their lines, preceded by two or three words of their cue. In the Elizabethan playhouse the parts were formed into scrolls, so Bottom, as the lead, gets a fat scroll, Flute gets a thinner one, and Snug, who must roar extempore, gets no scroll at all. But it is Bottom who has the last line in the scene, even though it may not make immediate sense to a modern audience (and requires a deal of explanation from modern editors).

This group of actors, although amateur, has some echoes of Shakespeare's own professional playing company, many members of which were originally tradesmen. James Burbage, theatre impresario, entrepreneur and father of Richard (who might have been playing one of the lovers) was himself a joiner. There seems little doubt, too, that Shakespeare is drawing directly on his own experience of rehearsal. See A. B. Taylor's fascinating essay that suggests that, in Quince, Shakespeare might be offering a gently satirical portrait of himself and his playwriting and, in Bottom, having a good humoured dig at Will Kempe, the Chamberlain's leading clown who most likely played the weaver. For an amusing and informative discussion of the existence of amateur players such as these in Shakespeare's times and since, and the durability of their play, see Michael Dobson's essay. Both are in Further Reading. So far as the plot is concerned, while we may have been puzzled at first by the switch from the court to this workshop, we will have begun to see a pattern of links emerging between the play of Pyramus and Thisbe (to be performed at Theseus' wedding) and the story of crossed lovers, thwarted by their parents, that has started to unfold in scene one. Hermia and Lysander, we know, will also meet in the wood, that night, 'a league [three miles] without the town' (I.i.165). The planning of the 'lamentable tragedy' has diverted us, briefly, from that trajectory, but the Athens Amateur Dramatic Society's plans to rehearse, that night, in the same wood, under Duke's oak, alerts us to the fact that the wood is becoming the focus of the action, the attempt to frustrate young love the core of the theme.

Act II

Act II, scene i

The play now moves from the city to the wood, from day to night, from the mortal to the fairy world. It is a shift from the controlling structures of the court to the freedom of the forest, nurture to nature. The contrast between city – or court – and country is one Shakespeare draws on frequently, in comedies (such as Love's Labour's Lost and As You Like It), tragedies (King Lear) and the late plays (The Winter's Tale, The Tempest). In modern performances, with our sense of the distinction between these worlds being less clearly defined than in Shakespeare's day, delineating them on stage can present specific problems – the sheep-shearing in Act IV of The Winter's Tale is a case in point. In the Elizabethan open-air public playhouse, with no break to speak of in the action, and no elaborate stage effects to call on, Shakespeare sets and sustains his location primarily through language, while later productions have seized the opportunity to create the wood in line with the overall scenography of the performance and their own time's theatrical fashion (see Chapter 4 for examples).

0 *Enter a* **Fairy** *at one door and* **Robin Goodfellow [Puck]** *at another* The Quarto stage direction indicates the use of the doors each side of the stage of the playhouse as an unnamed Fairy comes face to face with another sprite who is, to the audience, as yet unidentified. Robin is, in fact, another name for Puck, and is used for many speech-headings in the Quarto and Folio texts. A puck is a generic name for any mischievous goblin, but this is the name by which the character is generally known, and will be throughout the Commentary. The character of Robin Goodfellow appeared in an anonymous play, *Grim, the Collier of Croydon*, staged a few years after *A Midsummer Night's Dream*, 'in a suit of leather close to his body; his face and hands russet-colour, with a flail' – a club-like instrument for threshing corn.

1–17 The first line suggests Puck encounters the Fairy on his (or her; though the original actor would have been male) way to do something. The verse forms will immediately strike us as different from anything used so far in the play and continue Shakespeare's display of virtuoso writing. The Fairy begins with four lines, each made up of two pairs of three-syllable phrases, unstressed-unstressed-stressed (ŏ-vĕr híll, ŏ-vĕr dale), known as an *anapaestic* pattern, which are internally rhymed (dale/pale, briar/fire) and alliterative. The following eight lines each comprises eight syllables, and are again rhymed, though the first pair (where/sphere) is not an immediate rhyme to our ears. Try speaking these lines, and it becomes apparent how they give a sense of speed and purpose, and how the strong and effective contrast they provide with the previous scene helps establish the change in place and mood. The last three lines of the Fairy's speech shift into regular, rhyming, iambic pentameters, which are picked up by Puck. The shifting structure of the language reflects the freedom enjoyed by the spirit world and by this servant of Titania ('I do wander everywhere') compared with the strictures and constraints of the court and city. The flowers listed by the fairy evoke Titania's retinue of fairies as a miniature version of Elizabeth I's personal bodyguard of 50 handsome young gentlemen-pensioners in gold coats, lines designed to stress the status of both mortal and fairy Queen. With a casual dismissal of Puck as a lob (lout), the First Fairy warns him of Titania's imminent arrival.

18–31 To match the Fairy Queen there is a Fairy King – Oberon, who is planning to come to this self-same spot – and just as there is conflict between lovers in the mortal world of Theseus' court, so there is dissent between these two monarchs. The cause of their quarrel is a 'lovely boy, stolen from an Indian king': Oberon wants the boy to engage with him in manly pursuits as a 'Knight of his train', while Titania 'crowns him with flowers'.

32–59 The Fairy (who presumably knows all this) has worked out from this other spirit's appearance and demeanour that he is Robin Goodfellow, a 'knavish sprite' who delights in mischief-making. Puck doesn't deny it, and the actor might see opportunities in his speech (lines 42–57) to embellish the lines with physical action and vocal tricks, and to imitate the accents of country people.

Enter **Oberon** *the King of Fairies, at one door, with his train, and* **Titania** *the Queen, at another, with hers.*

59 This is a formal entrance and the use of the doors suggests the confrontation as the two fairy monarchs 'square' (line 30) up to each other, visually an image of this battle of the sexes. Titania's train presumably includes the Fairy already on stage, as well as Peaseblossom, Cobweb, Moth and Mustardseed. The members of Oberon's train are not specified, but presumably are of a similar number. This entrance also echoes that of Theseus and Hippolyta at the start of the play – the more so if the roles of the spirit and mortal rulers are doubled.

60–80 The arrival of Oberon and Titania is marked by a further change in the verse form, from rhyming couplets to blank verse. ('Titania' is probably intended by Shakespeare to be pronounced with the first syllable to rhyme with 'tight' and the last three with 'mania'.) Titania's reference to Oberon having come from 'the farthest step of India', added to the earlier mention of the 'Indian king' (line 22) may suggest that India is these fairies' home (and that has influenced their presentation in a number of productions; see Chapter 4). But these are not remote, otherworldly figures; their robust exchanges have the vigour of a squabble between any human couple who are disaffected with each other. They acknowledge their married state, but Titania accuses Oberon of making love to other women by assuming the guise of a pastoral lover. Indeed, she claims his purpose in turning up now is to bless the wedding of Theseus to Hippolyta who, she reveals with a disdainful tone, was once Oberon's 'bouncing' (meaning 'strapping' or 'swaggering') and 'buskined mistress' (lines 70–1). 'Buskins' are half-length boots, and this is possibly a clue as to how Hippolyta was originally costumed. But 'buskined' was also used in Shakespeare's time as shorthand for a tragic demeanour, which is interesting to consider in the context of Hippolyta's mood in the opening scene of the play. Oberon doesn't deny the charges, but retaliates with the accusation that Titania was Theseus' lover, and stole him from the (many) other women to whom he had pledged himself. (Maybe this explains why Theseus was so keen to move on when Lysander mentioned that Demetrius had been two-timing Hermia with Helena?) It's worth noting that while the 'flowery train' of women's names will be unlikely to mean much to modern readers or spectators, for some in Shakespeare's time the inclusion in the list of 'Antiopa' will have recalled the role of Theseus as the 'ravisher' of the Amazon queen and work 'as allusive poetry properly works, as a series of casements opening on the wild foam of European story' (Nuttall 2000, p. 51).

81–117 Titania describes this – very English – world as, in the words of the poet John Keats, 'something rich and luxurious', creating for us, in our minds, the physical and sensual natural world inhabited by these spirits. Good dancing is often used as an emblem of cohesion and harmony in early modern plays, and while Titania and her train wish to dance in peace, they are constantly disrupted by the 'brawls' (vigorous and noisy dances) of Oberon and his crew. But, most significantly, Titania identifies their personal domestic crisis, their inability to let each other live in peace, as the direct cause of the earthly and cosmic disorder: the rivers have broken their banks, making the fields impossible to plough and rotting the corn before it ripens for harvest. Drawing more and more detailed examples (and showing an understanding for the suffering of the mortal world that is not typical of Elizabethan attitudes to fairies), she describes how sheep and cattle die of disease or drown in the floods, becoming food only for carrion, while the places for rural sports and pastimes are destroyed. People suffer in summer the weather and ailments of winter, but enjoy none of the cheer or customs of winter, and frost kills the roses and new buds. People are terrified by this chaos, and all is because of the 'dissent' between her and Oberon. Titania's long speech (the longest in the play so far) does not advance the play's narrative, and is often (I think wrongly) shortened in performance. It expounds a core idea in the play that individual passions can overturn order, allow control of society and nature to be lost, and lead to confusion and disaster. The natural world is both a force of good and beauty but is also one that can threaten the safety and the wellbeing of humans and spirits alike.

118–37 For Oberon, the solution to their quarrel and its effects is in her hands: she should give up the boy. But Titania – who is, as far as we know, childless herself – now reveals, in a speech of great beauty, the relationship she has with the child, and had with his mother, who died in childbirth. The image of the relationship of the two women, in the 'spicèd Indian air' – one a spirit, the other mortal, one the mistress the other her maid – with the mother-to-be likened to a ship in full, billowing sail, is the first expression we have encountered so far of genuine, unthreatened pleasure two people can take in each other's company, and makes a telling contrast with the self-interested competitiveness or imposed constraint that has dominated relationships to date. It recalls the description Helena has given of her close friendship with Hermia, and it is not uncommon for Shakespeare to see relationships between people of the same sex as those that produce the greatest mutual affection.

Although he has no part to play on stage and no lines to say, many productions and film versions choose to include the character of the Indian boy, and where the role is played by an older youth, to hint, as many critics have done also, at a level of sexual interest in him on the part of both Titania and Oberon. Others have seen the boy as 'a symbol of what Oberon really desires, the gift of Titania's love and obedience' (Calderwood 1992, p. 55). In almost all instances where he appears on stage, however, the character is presented as non-European, non-white, and post-colonial critical perspectives have placed him within the context of Elizabethan trade and exploration as something to be bartered – 'Indian ware', for example, was a contemporary term for rare and exotic goods, sought-after commodities – and have identified the 'language of trade' that Shakespeare employs in Titania's description of both the mother and her child (Penguin edition 2005, pp. xxxix–xl), though see my comments on what I would term the 'language of affection' in that passage, too.

138–45 Just how little Oberon is touched by Titania's words is made clear in his peremptory enquiry about her plans, which she adroitly but equally abruptly turns aside with a rhyme. She invites him to join her and her followers (presumably with little expectation he will accept) if he will be patient, and to dance with them – both images of harmony – but he makes it clear he will only do so if he gets the boy. Before she loses her temper with him even more, she exits with her train, having the last word on a rhyme.

146–76 Oberon plans his revenge for the 'injury' Titania has done him, further suggesting that her love for, and possession of, the

Indian boy has particular significance for him. Titania has recalled her votaress, and now Oberon remembers his 'imperial votaress'. Calling Puck to him, he describes, in a lyrical speech (often thought to refer to Queen Elizabeth and to a celebration in her honour, so reaching out from the play's fictional world to that of its audience; see Chapters 1 and 3), how an arrow fired at her by Cupid, missed its mark, and fell upon a flower, love in idleness (which we now call a wild pansy), staining its whiteness with purple. This flower has the magical power, when put upon the eyes of someone sleeping, to make them 'madly dote' on who, or what, they first see on waking. Puck is despatched to the other side of the world to find the flower.

177–87   Oberon is left alone on stage (his train presumably having been dismissed, probably immediately following Titania's departure). In soliloquy, he shares with us his plans, listing animals known for their fierceness or sexual potency and more appropriate for a jungle or wild forest than the bucolic English countryside setting conjured up so far. At the sound of people approaching he announces he is invisible. The records of the Elizabethan theatrical impresario, Philip Henslowe, note that his company possessed 'a robe for to go invisible', while subsequent productions have devised their own signifiers. Of course, on a stage, if a character tells you he's invisible, and no one sees him, he is.

Enter Demetrius, Helena *following him*

187–244   The arrival of Demetrius 'pursued' by Helena suggests the speed of their entrance, and as they too squabble over another person (Hermia) we hear something of the acerbic tone of the previous part of the scene with Oberon and Titania. But we will also compare this scene with the tender one between Lysander and Hermia earlier, and realise that Helena did indeed carry out her plan to tell Demetrius that the lovers had fled into the wood. The vigour of the scrap between Helena and Demetrius demands that the lines should be played quickly, but it's not always easy to pick up their meaning at that playing speed. For example, we might miss Helena's extended mix of images and proverbial sayings that move from the idea of iron being attracted by a magnet (the 'adamant' of line 195) to that of her heart as something softer than iron but still as 'true as steel'. Of course, it may be that that is exactly the effect Shakespeare intends: of Helena rather over-dramatising herself and her situation. As she abases herself before Demetrius, he reminds her (and us) that this is not the city but an inhospitable, remote and dangerous place for a young woman to be at night, especially in the company of one who may wish her harm, an argument she swiftly turns aside. He, like Oberon, threatens to expose this woman he cannot command to the 'wild beasts' of the forest, but she throws back at him how he is forcing her to invert normal behaviour (an echo of Titania's speech) through his own, abnormal, attitude, and that he behaves badly to her in temple, town and country. When Demetrius exits with a final threat (her rhyme emphasising his departure), she continues this sense of reversal in her closing rhyming couplet, directly echoing Hermia's earlier complaint (I.i.207) that Demetrius has turned 'a heaven unto a hell'.

245–end of scene　　Oberon is alone on stage for two lines, and, having watched from the sidelines, decides to reverse their situation. That brief solitary moment must not be intruded on, as it is essential that the audience knows that Puck, entering now, does not see or hear the exchanges between Helena and Demetrius. Far from the 'desert place' (line 218) or the dangerous forest suggested by his earlier lines (lines 180–1), the image Oberon now conjures up in this famous speech is much closer to how we might imagine an English wood, and it may begin to be apparent to us that this place (rather like the playhouse stage itself) is defined each time by the inner state of mind or imagination of the characters themselves. Oberon's specific and detailed words create in our mind's eye a place of some beauty, shaded from the sun and filled with 'luscious' scented flowers gently 'nodding' in the breeze, with a friendly snake (not the usual threatening serpent) who sloughs her skin to provide clothes for fairies. But at line 258 Oberon's lines suddenly shift to reveal an undercurrent of violence in this Eden, with his wish that Titania should have 'hateful fantasies'. At this moment, the plots are further interlinked as Oberon decides that while he attends to his wife, Puck should use the rest of the juice on the 'disdainful youth' wearing the 'Athenian garments'. Oberon, of course, means Demetrius, but the vague description he offers may suggest to us the possible confusion that might ensue, despite Puck's confident closing assurances to his master.

Act II, scene ii

0 *Enter* **Titania,** *Queen of Fairies, with her train*   The action follows on immediately from the previous scene, transporting us to the spot so evocatively described by Oberon, where Titania and her retinue presumably seek some peace and quiet after her quarrel with her husband.

1–8   While Titania, Oberon and (possibly) Puck appear to be conceived as adult figures, the other fairies, although they are ferocious – they 'kill' and 'make war' and defend their mistress – are clearly to be imagined as small enough to climb into rose buds, make coats from bats wings, and so on. Indeed, this apparent discrepancy between their fictional size and that of actors has been the subject of critical debate and for some critics in earlier periods even raised questions of the viability of the play on stage.

9–30   Apart from the general instruction that 'Fairies sing', the quartos and Folio indicate that a First Fairy (presumably the same fairy who encountered Puck at the opening of II.i) sings at line 20, joined by a second fairy at line 31, though it is not clear exactly how much they sing alone, and most editions divide the lines as first suggested by the editor, Edward Capell, in 1767. While they sing, the fairies presumably dance a 'roundel' (called for by Titania in I.i) which is both a traditional English country-dance – a circle dance – and a simple song. Here it is a lullaby, with a refrain (suggesting again that it is the Warwickshire countryside and its ways that Shakespeare has in mind; see the discussion of Granville Barker's production, pp. 112–14). In comparison with the large beasts Oberon lists as sees inhabiting the forest, these are smaller woodland creatures – snakes, hedgehogs, spiders, beetles, worms and snails. Perceiving such animals as a threat is in line with the fairies' diminutive size, but while we now know them to be harmless, in Shakespeare's day they were generally believed to be venomous: there *are* dangers in this place.

The fairies' invitation to Philomel (the nightingale, a bird famed for the beauty of its song) to join with their lullaby is, as we have noted with many other aspects of the play, double-edged. The reference is to the story of Philomel (told by Ovid in his *Metamorphoses*), who was turned into a bird after being raped and mutilated by Tereus,

her brother-in-law, who was himself punished by being turned into
a hoopoe (a bird with striking plumage). Shakespeare had used the
story in *Titus Andronicus*, to comment on the fate of Titus' daughter,
Lavinia, who is raped in a threatening forest. Given Oberon's threats
to torment Titania with erotic and 'hateful fantasies', this echo of
Philomel's story within the contrasting frame of the soothing song
may strike us as ominous.

30 SD *Titania sleeps* presumably on the herb and flower decked 'bank'
to which Oberon referred earlier. (The Admiral's Men, a rival company
to Shakespeare's, list two moss banks among their properties.)

31–2 Although the quartos also indent these lines, suggesting they
too are sung, modern editions frequently treat them as dialogue. The
Fairies exit, leaving one (the First Fairy?) to stand 'aloof' – a word commonly used in stage-directions to indicate 'at a respectful distance'– as
a guard.

Enter Oberon

33–40 In performance, Oberon's attendants frequently capture
the fairy guard, before he anoints Titania's eyes. Oberon's spell –
or curse, rather – is, like many speeches by the fairies, in seven
syllable lines with a stressed beat followed by an unstressed, the
gentle rhythm and rhymes contrasting with the image the words
themselves create of the forest as a place of wild and dangerous
animals. With his ultimate and disturbing desire that it should be
'some vile thing' that attracts his wife, Oberon exits.

*But what happens to Titania? Breaking my rule about not looking ahead:
she doesn't wake up until III.i.122, some 253 lines away, during which
time, once the potion is administered, she plays no part in the action and
does not need to remain visible. She could exit (clumsy perhaps), or be concealed in some way. On the Elizabethan stage she might have withdrawn
into the recess of a central entrance, if there were one, while in modern performances she is frequently raised up above the stage. Alternatively, she
might remain on the stage (especially if there's no break between acts two
and three), fully visible to us but unseen by the mortals as they stumble
through the wood.*

41–71 *Enter* **Lysander** *and* **Hermia,** lost and tired from 'wandering in the woods' in search of his aunt (assuming she ever existed). The verse shifts for four lines from couplets to alternately rhymed lines, before reverting to couplets, suggesting the affectionate and playful mood between them. Lysander's verbal dexterity is quickly employed to try to get Hermia to let him lie down next to her, but she sees through him: as she says – the line standing out as a non-rhyme in the midst of a flow of couplets – 'Lysander riddles very prettily' (line 59). The lines, constantly punning on different meanings of 'lie' (and on the first syllable of his name, too), indicate the staging: 'this bank' is where she will lie to sleep (is Titania asleep on it too?), but he wants to share 'one turf' of it too; her instruction to 'lie further off' countered by his desire (does he do it?) to lie down side by side with her, until he obeys her instruction to 'lie further off', and agrees that 'here' (perhaps she indicates exactly how far he must be 'distant') is where his bed is. They say goodnight to each other with her wish, and his promise, that his love and loyalty to her will never change.

Enter Puck

72–89 The similarities between Lysander and Demetrius begin to pay comic dividends here, as Puck (who, we recall, did not witness the exchanges between Demetrius and Helena) comes across the sleeping Lysander, dressed in the 'weeds of Athens' he's been told to look out for: like all good comedy, the jokes and business need a believable foundation. Looking at the couple, Puck spectacularly misreads the situation: to him, Hermia is a 'despised maid' asleep on 'dank and dirty ground', too frightened to lie nearer to this 'churl' who has rejected her. Puck's line 83 has two extra syllables, signalling his move to squeezing the juice in Lysander's eyes, uttering the spell that will, he thinks, put all right.

89–108 As Puck exits, leaving the lovers sleeping, he does not see Demetrius and Helena enter, 'running', she still in pursuit of him. Her word 'darkling' (meaning 'in the dark', here both literally and figuratively) reminds us that (originally at least) the scene, though played in daylight is set at night, and we will need to bear that in mind while reading. It explains why they don't spot the other lovers or (depending on the staging) Titania. Demetrius' and Helena's exchange, full of verbs as vigorous as their mood and cut short by Demetrius' exit, shifts in Helena's soliloquy (she is, to all intents and purposes, alone on stage as everyone else is asleep), from unrhymed to rhymed couplets. Her tendency to do herself down sees her compare herself unfavourably with Hermia and liken herself, now she is in the forest, to a bear, a monster, ugly enough to scare away even the other animals, let alone Demetrius. Her self-pity is interrupted as, moving around in the dark, she bumps into a body on the ground and has to get close to it before she can identify it as that of a sleeping – or even dead – Lysander.

109–40   The suddenness of Lysander's waking, and of his equally instant infatuation with Helena, is conveyed by his completing the rhyme of the couplet, and he continues in the same mode (his elaborate and, even in Shakespeare's day, rather archaic phrase, 'sphery eyne', being entirely in keeping with his poetic inclinations). His immediate thought is for Demetrius. Why? It's almost as if he's been transported back to the first scene, but with Helena now the focus of their rivalry. Helena offers a good reason for him to calm down – whether Demetrius loves Hermia or not is of no consequence: what matters, is that Hermia loves Lysander. We know of course that Lysander is subject to the potion, his actions controlled by supernatural forces, but ironically he invokes his reason – three times – to explain his (irrational) affection for Helena: it is because he has grown up, has put his youthful errors aside and because his affections have now found their true object. He signs off with what again sound suspiciously like a couple of lines from one of his own love poems. Indeed, perhaps it is that, added to the sheer speed of his conversion and her likely previous experience of his mocking tongue (as we heard in I.i), that alerts Helena to the possibility that she's being played with. More to the point, Lysander has never before, so far as we know, expressed any amorous interest in Helena; as we saw in the opening scene, he and Hermia only had eyes for each other. Helena's response is firm, measured and dignified, her repeated phrases giving the lines strength and fluency (they are still couplets, though a modern actor will probably lose the rhyme of 'eye/insufficiency'), with her exit lines allowing her an opportunity to share her plight with the audience.

141–50   The strength of the spell Lysander's under (and the fact that it *is* a spell) is conveyed by the surprising violence of his language; he sees Hermia as a 'surfeit' and a 'heresy', a source of 'deepest loathing' and things 'hated' (which makes him sound just like Oberon wishing for Titania to wake when some 'vile thing' approached). As he exits he casts himself in a heroic mode – a valiant knight pledging himself to his true love: Helena.

151–end of scene   Earlier, the fairies sang a charm to keep the sleeping Titania safe from the forest's 'spotted snakes with double tongue' (II.ii.9). Hermia seems at first to speak while still dreaming, trying to wake up, and gradually coming out of a dream in which – as if the violence of Lysander's words has penetrated her sleep – a snake tried to 'eat her heart' while Lysander looked on smiling. As well as revealing her intuition of bodily harm – the snake as a phallic symbol might also suggest her confused sexual emotions – it also expresses the dark and irrational nature of dreaming that is vital to an understanding of the forest experience (Garber 1974, p. 7; Holland 1994), and her use of the word 'serpent' will again suggest a topsy-turvy Eden. Her fear is mixed with comedy (and we'll be clear by now that this is a blend the play engages in) as she moves abruptly (changes are sudden in this wood) from maidenly distress to a practical, commonsense solution to her situation.

Throughout this scene Shakespeare has again used various patterns of language to reflect the range of emotions experienced by the characters. Accordingly, while the passion and the dangers they face are all consuming to the characters, they are observed more coolly by us, with the detachment of comedy rather than the engagement of tragedy. The plot lines of the young mortal lovers and the older spirit ones have begun to be linked. With the quarrel between Titania and Oberon it is almost as if the tensions that lurk in the sub-text of the opening scene's exchanges between Theseus and Hippolyta have surfaced in the more liberating atmosphere of the wood. Interestingly enough, although the play itself, and characters' experiences within it, may be seen by them as a dream (Bottom's night with Titania, the lovers' experiences in the wood, for example), Hermia's dream is, in fact, the only actual dream in the play.

Act III

Act III, scene i

Although the Folio text introduced act breaks where there had been none in the quartos, the location of the stage remains broadly the same (though we know the mechanicals planned to rehearse at the Duke's Oak), and Titania, if she is still onstage – concealed or in view – remains asleep.

0 Enter the Clowns *The quarto stage direction embraces all the actors playing the mechanicals under the one term: clowns. In the Elizabethan theatre, and even more so in its earlier years, the clowns, specialist comic actors, were stars whose fame and popularity matched – even, in the case of superstars like Richard Tarlton, outstripped – that of the serious actors. Marlowe may have opened Tamburlaine with a clarion call to defeat the notion of a theatre kept 'in pay' by 'clownage', and we might with reason think we hear something of Shakespeare's own frustrations when Hamlet talks of the need to restrain the comedians. But the term 'clowns' reminds us of the considerable vocal and physical skills these actors brought to their parts, able, with a perfectly timed line, or a well-judged gesture or look to the audience, to set the playhouse in a roar. Of course, we can today often (though perhaps less so in this particular play) find Shakespeare's jokes obscure when we read them: Edmund Blackadder (Rowan Atkinson's creation), meeting Shakespeare on a time-travelling journey, memorably hit him in reprisal for imposing his dead jokes on subsequent generations. But it is astonishing how often, in the hands of a skilful actor, speaking and performing can bring alive what may seem inert on the page. Not always, of course. Some humour will remain hidden behind the varnish of many centuries, and stubbornly refusing to cut such lines will only result in a deflating scene: you can't necessarily act a footnote.*

1–5   Ever assertive, Bottom speaks first. As the company search out a good spot to rehearse, Shakespeare plays on a neat inversion of Elizabethan theatre practice. Usually, early modern plays invite us to imagine that the permanent physical structure of the stage represents something quite different (the prologue to *Henry V* is a good example, when the spectators are asked to use their imaginations to overcome the deficiencies of stage and staging). Here, however, we are invited to go one step further: to imagine the actual tiring house is a 'hawthorn brake' and the stage a 'green plot', and once having done that, to envisage that that imaginary hawthorn bush is a tiring house, the grass a stage.

6–24   Quince's 'bully Bottom' suggests that friendly relations have been restored after their slightly strained dealings in their previous scene. But Quince might be about to be tested again. Having had time since the parts were allotted to read the play, Bottom has become deeply concerned as to its suitability for the occasion. To begin with, and confident of how convincing a performance he will deliver, he fears that drawing a sword in the performance will alarm the women in the audience; there's probably the same bawdy allusion (sword=penis) that I noted in scene one, though again used unintentionally on the character's part. Bottom's solution (which has the added bonus of giving him more to do: he even wants more syllables in the lines than Quince offers) is to suggest he should speak a prologue to assure the audience that the death is just make-believe.

25–42   Bottom's concerns are catching, and now it's Tom Snout, who is emerging as a rather nervous man, a prophet of doom, expressing concerns about the lion. Snout thinks another prologue might be needed, but, as ever, Bottom has a solution, which again rests on undermining the convincing illusion he believes they will achieve: Snug should have a costume that reveals his face, and lines be written for him that confirm he's not really a lion. Snug, self-confessed as 'slow of study', may silently look on, viewing the growth of his part with less confident enthusiasm than Bottom does that of his own.

There's an issue here that will need to be resolved before rehearsals begin, since re-allocating lines once actors have them (especially if they've not got many in the first place) can be a tricky business. In the quartos, the speech headings in this scene have 'Sno' and 'Sn', presumably indicating Snout and Snug. In the second Folio, however, the heading 'Sn' at line 46 is expanded to Snout, leaving Snug with no lines at all in the scene. In fact, as well as leaving line 39 to Snug, there might be some comic potential if he, as the member of the company most likely to have to build this bit of scenery, is the one who confidently asserts 'You can never bring in a wall' (59). Alternatively, if Snug were to remain silent in this scene, his performance later might come as more of a surprise.

43–55   As in all early rehearsals (and even more in this case with a
new play by a presumably novice playwright) time has to be spent in
sorting out the practicalities of the performance. Quince has clearly
been struggling with 'two hard things' (line 43) in the staging. First,
how can they convincingly present 'moonlight'? Shakespeare has,
of course, been doing precisely that through much of the play up
till now, and doing it through a characteristically Elizabethan combination of language, the actors' performances and the unspoken
contract with the audience that they will on their 'imaginary forces
work' (*Henry V*, Prologue, 18). Here, however, having ascertained
from a calendar (Quince just happens to have one with him) that the
moon will, as we already know, be full on the wedding night, they
speculate that they could leave a window open for the moonlight to
shine through. But Quince, perhaps affected by the earlier solutions
to scenic problems, proposes a more overtly theatrical solution: that
they should have someone portray, or 'figure' (represent) the Man in
the Moon (or 'disfigure' him, as Quince says, maybe speaking more
accurately than he knows; note the echo with Theseus' use of the
word in I.i.151 and see Weimann 2000, pp. 80–8). There is quite a
confusion of theatrical styles brewing here: a (probably misplaced)
fear of things being too 'real' in the performance mixed with an
emblematic style of representation that would have been perfectly at
home in the earlier Tudor drama.

55–69   Next: the wall. Evidently not having seen Shakespeare's
most recent solution to a wall – the orchard wall in Act II scene i of
Romeo and Juliet – the amateur troupe build on their idea to use an
actor, suitably decorated with lime and gravel plaster, to solve this
challenging staging issue. Bottom indicates that as well as being
covered in building materials, Wall should hold his fingers 'thus' –
though it's left to the actor to decide exactly how that is – to represent
the chink through which the lovers speak. Quince is clearly not con-
vinced that they will manage this, but – the procrastinating over that
marks all rehearsals before the first line actually has to be spoken – he
calls them to order, reminds them of the set and entrances, and the
rehearsal at last commences.

69 SD *Enter Puck*   But before they get going, Puck (who is, of course,
invisible to mortals) enters. In fact, the Folio has an earlier entrance for

Puck in addition to this one, at line 41 (which is preferred by the Oxford edition). The advantage of entering then would be that he could have observed them for a moment or two before he speaks; the disadvantage would be if his entrance took the focus from the energetic discussion about moonshine that's going on at that point.

70–3 Puck's sneeringly superior reference to the amateur actors as 'hempen homespuns' tells us a bit about how Shakespeare imagined they might be dressed as well as their general demeanour. Puck also reminds us (which is especially necessary if she is not visible) of the nearby presence of the sleeping Titania in – we are asked to imagine – her fairy-sized cradle.

Actors (certainly professional ones) don't on the whole much like being watched in rehearsal by outsiders. Quince's cast have two audiences now – ourselves, and Puck – and his presence subtly but significantly shifts our perspective to that of watchers watching someone watching.

74–80 This is the first time we have heard Quince's play and though it has some virtues – a variety of verse forms, a good strong story of love denied and a tragic ending; rather like *A Midsummer Night's Dream*, in fact, apart from the outcome – things don't get off to a great start. Quince (calling Thisbe to 'stand forth', the same phrase that introduced Lysander and Demetrius in the opening scene) has to interrupt Bottom even before he completes his first line. It is not clear whether they are reading from their parts or if they have learned their lines, but Bottom either misreads or has mislearnt his script. In fact, editors have pondered over what's actually meant here. Some (the Norton and Oxford, for example) adopt the Folio reading – 'Odours. Odours.' – while other emendations include 'Odorous! Odorous!' and 'Odious. – odorous!' My choice would be to keep the quartos' reading ('Odours! Odorous!'), with Quince first repeating Bottom's mistake (a chance to get something of his own back?) before giving him the correct reading (making the most of the size and rolling shape of the word), which Bottom gets wrong again, but differently this time – no doubt to Quince's despair.

81 As Puck follows Bottom into the tiring-house/hawthorn brake, he must immediately pick up Bottom's exit line, as his rhyme to complete the couplet clearly indicates that he conceives his trick at this precise moment.

82–95 Back on stage, Quince's guidance to Flute is not as clear as an actor – especially an inexperienced – one might hope, and Flute, overcome with nerves, begins to speak, no doubt trying to affect a female voice and manner. In this respect, the actor in Shakespeare's theatre had a more difficult task than his modern counterpart. There, the audience had already in this play seen young men playing the parts of Hippolyta, Titania, Hermia and Helena, and doing so, I'm certain, in a restrained and (within the convention) convincing manner. There are no instances in this play – as there are in *Twelfth Night* and *As You Like It*, for example – where a boy plays a girl playing a boy, so foregrounding a wealth of possibilities for sexual and gender confusion. Under the stern gaze stare of his director, Flute understandably panics and speaks all his lines at once, including, according to Quince, his cues (see Pettitt 2007, pp. 220–3). It seems that Thisbe's 'part' reads as follows:

cue: *... to thee appear.*
Thisbe: Most radiant Pyramus, most lilywhite of hue,
Of colour like the red rose on triumphant briar,
Most brisky juvenal, and eke most lovely Jew,
As true as truest horse that never yet would tire.
        Cue: *... were only thine.*
Thisbe: I'll meet thee, Pyramus, at Ninus' tomb.

In fact, they never get to do the sequence properly: Flute moves in and out of character, mispronounces 'Ninus' (the legendary founder of the ancient city of Nineveh) as 'Ninny' (a fool – the same joke works today), all to the annoyance of Quince, whose exasperation is carried effortlessly for the actor by the colloquial rhythm of his lines.

96–107 Bottom's entrance, 'with the ass-head', brings everything to a halt (the 'fair' applies to Bottom, not Thisbe, which given his appearance, enhances the joke). It is, of course, a show-stopping moment (and I have seen Thisbe pass clean out with the shock of the sight of him). I've referred in Chapter 3 to the range of sources for this moment and in Chapter 6 to the critical responses to the cultural and sexual associations with the ass. In Bottom in his ass head, Shakespeare creates one of the two (the other is Hamlet and the skull) great iconic moments of classical English theatre. More immediately, the shock that Bottom's appearance delivers to his fellow actors provides great opportunities for a comic exit, with the mechanicals harried by Puck, apparently imitating the sounds (and movements?) of horses, hounds (in one production he cocked his leg as if to urinate over the audience), hogs and a 'headless bear'.

For the actor who's playing Bottom, the effect on his performance of wearing the head (assuming it even partially covers his face) will be marked. In the same way that actors performing in a mask talk of the ways it liberates characteristics entirely different from themselves, so actors who have played Bottom talk of the impact of the head: the animal characteristics merging with the human character, and vice versa, drawing out parts of each to create something new. F. Murray Abraham (Bottom in Joe Papp's 1987 production), for example, has written that 'when I put on that ass's head I felt instantly potent, randy, and very, very attractive'. Of course, there are as many realisations of the ass's head as there are performances, from frameworks that merely suggest the ass to more or less realistic replica heads with eyes and ears moved by strings or, more recently, electronics. David Wiles argues that in the Elizabethan theatre a 'fool's cap with ears was used', which could have been 'held up as cuckold's horns when Bottom at the end of the song becomes the "cuckoo"' (1998, p. 78). Whatever solution a performance finds, I suspect most actors would undoubtedly prefer some kind of half-mask, leaving their mouths and, crucially, their eyes, free.

108–29   Disoriented by fear, Snout finds himself back in the glade. Quince returns, too, though maybe he's come back to retrieve the precious copy of the play. His term for what has happened to Bottom – that he's been 'translated' – is entirely appropriate, for, apart from meaning to be turned into something else (often a beast) it was used specifically by Elizabethan craftsmen – especially tailors and cobblers – to refer to making something new and different out of remnants.

Bottom, unaware of his 'translation', thinks he is the victim of a practical joke by his fellow cast members; indeed, his sudden rebuke to Snout at 108–9 may suggest Snout is gesturing to indicate to Bottom what's happened. But, like others in the wood before him have found, this is not a place where one necessarily wants to be alone. To raise his spirits and show them he's not afraid, he starts to sing (weavers were evidently known for their singing). With its clutch of woodland birds, perhaps it was an echo of a song Shakespeare knew from his boyhood in the Stratford countryside. Titania, earlier lulled to sleep by the harmonious roundel of her fairies, is now woken by Bottom's stentorian singing. But as she catches sight of him and, in an echo of Lysander's wakening earlier, her eyes too are charmed and she sees not an ass but an angel. It is not clear whether Bottom sees or hears her just yet, but he launches into a second verse, its closing word – 'nay' – undoubtedly a cue to the actor to let his donkey persona emerge.

130–40 Titania speaks in verse, Bottom in prose. Although, as in this instance, the presence of these forms can indicate differences in status between characters, there are many other reasons why they a dramatist might employ them. Here, for example, they also differentiate between mortal and spirit, ethereal and earthy. It isn't, in my experience, always easy in the theatre to *hear* the difference between verse and prose (as I assume Elizabethans could), but here the distinction is clear, with Titania's mellifluous lines, confessing that, for her, though it's love at first sight, it is nevertheless love based on convincing reasons, countered by Bottom's rather blunt common sense (remembering he still doesn't realise he *looks* different). Indeed, his observation that 'reason and love keep little company together nowadays' is, in different ways, as true of what we've seen of *all* the lovers in the play as it is of this new situation. While Titania's attitude is explained by the spell she's under, it's interesting, I think, to consider why Bottom shows no surprise at all when this supernatural creature suddenly appears to him.

141–91 For his part, Bottom, having exchanged pleasantries with Titania, is focused on getting out of the wood. Perhaps he tries to run away, but her spell stops him in his tracks. While gently requesting that he stay, she firmly removes any choice on his part, and tempts him with the sybaritic pleasures that will be his if he remains (though I think this is all verbal rather than physical caressing at this stage). Moving into rhyming couplets she summons her fairies and, in a speech every line of which rhymes with the one before, and which also carefully guide their actions, instructs them how to make Bottom comfortable, and to treat him like a 'gentleman' by doing him 'courtesies'. Bottom (still not fazed, it seems, by the fairies, who are small enough at one moment to steal the honey from the bee yet big enough at the next to carry figs and grapes) begins to make their acquaintance. His comments reveal a natural politeness and gentle wit, aspects of him we caught only glimpses of in the fraught circumstances of rehearsal.

192–end of scene　　Night is approaching, the dew is falling, and Titania is impatient to get Bottom to her bower. Her last line, with its instruction to 'tie up' Bottom's tongue (a hand over his mouth or something round his muzzle if he's wearing a full ass's head?) and to 'bring him silently' refers not to his amiable garrulousness, but, presumably to his excited and happy braying, while also reminding us of her superior status and authority over him (see Montrose 1995 for a discussion of hierarchies within the play). Titania's references to the moon and flowers 'lamenting some enforced (i.e., violated by force) chastity' does more than draw an image of the moon, Diana, as the goddess of chastity. It also, read slightly differently, reminds us of the plight of Hermia, who under Athenian law is being forced to remain chaste against her will, to escape which fate she too, at this moment, is wandering alone in the wood.

Act III, scene ii

1–34　　I have commented on the way the action in the wood flows easily from scene to scene, with little or no break in the action. Act III opens presumably somewhere else in the wood but at about the same moment that the previous scene between Bottom and Titania is concluding. What is interesting, therefore, is why Puck repeats for Oberon (who has of course not been there) the details of what we have just seen? It means there are problems for the actor of how to refresh the description to keep the audience interested. True, there are some details of the scattering of the terrified workmen that we might now choose to build in to the staging of that moment in the previous scene – such as the brilliant description of them like birds fleeing the hunter, or the chaos as they fall over each other in their haste to escape with cries of 'murder' – and Puck can no doubt do a good impression of Bottom, too. Or, as these details are new to us, might we suspect that Puck is embellishing his report? He must realise that he's rather overstepped his brief. *His* task was to anoint the young Athenian's eyes. Oberon was handling Titania, relying on some natural animal to come upon her and become the object of her love. In either case, why does Shakespeare do this? Some editors suggest that it indicates an interval. It's not Shakespeare's invariable practice to think it necessary to remind us of what we've seen and heard, but in our modern theatre, if an interval were to come at the end of III.i, this brief recap while an audience settles itself could be a bonus.

35–40   Maybe it is the detail and energy of Puck's recreation of the encounter in the glade that prompts Oberon to acknowledge that maybe Puck has improved upon his own original plan. Certainly, all appears to be going well, with Titania in love with a monster, and, according to Puck, the Athenian youth now in love with the right girl.

41–2   Demetrius and Hermia appear, the last combination of lovers, the one that Egeus would enforce, and the most unlikely among the humans. As Oberon withdraws in order to watch them (he seems to imply that he is at this point not invisible as he was earlier), Puck observes that it is the right woman – but not the right man. Is this an aside, not heard by Oberon? His apparent failure to respond might suggest it is, but it is possible that Oberon's reaction is cut off by Demetrius beginning to speak.

43–55   It is the first time the audience has seen this couple alone together. They speak in couplets, but it rapidly becomes clear that there is no rapport between them. There are other clues for the actors. Demetrius addresses Hermia as 'you', she calls him 'thou'. It's not a hard and fast rule with the Elizabethans, but generally, using 'you' implies a familiarity, whereas 'thou', intriguingly, can imply both familiarity and contempt. For example, in *Twelfth Night*, when Sir Toby, encouraging Sir Andrew to fight Sebastian, suggests that 'if thou thou'st him some thrice, it shall not be amiss' (III.i.43–4) he reveals his own contempt of Sir Andrew as well as of Sebastian. A modern audience won't be likely to pick up on these niceties but, as always, they can be useful to actors in informing the tone of their exchanges. Puck has reminded us that Bottom is 'translated', but Demetrius seems changed, too, drawing on language very different from the cold legal terms we got from him in the opening scene. Hermia is unchanged in her distrust of him, however (though her image of a hole big enough for the moon to creep through and displease her brother, the sun, by appearing on the other side of the earth at midday in the Antipodes, is unlikely to be immediately understood). Hermia is still uncertain whether or not Demetrius has killed Lysander, and whether or not (like Macbeth) he's in so deep that he might as well now kill her. Her line 'And kill me too', leaves six whole beats in the regular iambic pentameter, creating a significant pause while she waits for him to strike. To her, the only plausible reason for Lysander's absence is his death, her imagery linking with other metaphors of cosmic disorder when love's awry.

Throughout the play, the *actors* are challenged by the relationship between the forms of their language and the emotion the *character* must convey. Although Hermia's lines are in couplets, reading aloud will show how the sense needs to carry across the end of the line (and therefore across the rhyme) into the next line. Demetrius' lines, on the other hand, are largely end-stopped, confining him – a less mercurial figure than Hermia, or Lysander – to the structure of the verse.

56–87 Hermia interprets Demetrius' 'dead...grim' expression as confirmation of his guilt, while he sees it as the response to her cruelty. However, he has the wit to flatter her even at this moment by praising her beauty. But with Hermia impervious to his sweet-talking his earlier belligerence quickly returns, exposing his loathing for Lysander, and prompting again her desperate demands that he should tell her whether or not he has killed his rival. She seizes on her dream to recognise Demetrius as the snake about her heart and more of the old Demetrius surfaces when, having confessed he has not killed Lysander, he bargains over what she might give him if he tells her where Lysander is (something we know, of course, he has no idea about). Hermia, no doubt drawing herself up to her full height, scorns him and exits, leaving him thoroughly outclassed, out manoeuvred, and crushed. Worn out by the row and the chase, Demetrius – whose words (debt, bankrupt, owe, measure, pay,

tender) expose how he 'costs' experience as a business transaction –
becomes the third human lover to fall asleep in the wood.

88–99   The opportunity for Oberon to deliver a slow-burn look
to Puck, who is perhaps attempting to sidle off, will be too great
to resist. Brushing aside Puck's rather desperate defence of blam-
ing everything on men's fickleness in love, Oberon orders him to
find 'Helena of Athens' – he's being careful to give more precise
instructions this time – and 'by some illusion' (though we don't
know what that will be) bring her to this spot. He himself, meanwhile, taking no more chances on Puck's improvisatory skills, will
charm Demetrius' eyes.

100–1   Puck is undoubtedly keen to reassure his master of his
dedication to any task, but his petulant 'look how I go' may suggest
Oberon is ignoring him, perhaps annoyed, perhaps more concerned
now with trying to sort things out.

102–21   As soon as Oberon, speaking in couplets (though the
rhymes are not those of modern English) has put the love-juice in
Demetrius' eyes, Puck is back, elatedly reporting in rhyme which
captures his excitement (and relief?) the imminent arrival of Helena,
pursued by the love-sick Lysander. As he did when he came across
the mechanicals in the wood, Puck wants to be an audience of the
ensuing 'pageant' or play. As he and Oberon stand back (though they
are invisible), Puck relishes the confusion the plot of this play-within-a-play promises: note that the literal meaning of 'preposterous' is
with the rear at the front, a reversal of normality, and a key compo-
nent of comedy.

121 SD *Enter* Lysander *and* Helena – though Lysander will probably be following her as he earnestly pleads his case. After a fair few
hours wandering in the dark they are presumably looking rather
the worse for wear and, if they fail to notice the sleeping form of
Demetrius under their noses, both the sense of their obsession with
their own problems, and our fun, will be enhanced.

122–35   They speak in rhyme, Lysander vowing his love and, like the
best romantic lovers, whose actions and tones he no doubt displays,

doing so in tears. (Bottom earlier, we may remember, decided his performance of the thwarted lover Pyramus would require tears to convince the audience of his sincerity.) To Lysander, his tears are a sure sign of his fidelity; to Helena they are simply part of the trappings of a scheme to mock her. She remains certain (and why shouldn't she) that he really only loves Hermia. As often the case with Helena, her way of expressing her ideas is not always easy to grasp, especially if listened to at speed. Here, perhaps gestures of balancing one thing with another might help convey her notion that if Lysander were to swear an oath to Helena it would be simply cancelled out by his earlier vows to Hermia. But Lysander (who earlier argued for the need to arrive slowly at the correct judgement where love's concerned) now claims that his earlier choice of Hermia was misguided.

136–76   As I have noted, one of the powers of rhyme on stage is when it is interrupted. Here, the insertion of an unrhymed line (line 136) provides emphasis. More to the point it sets up the explosion of comedy as Demetrius wakes up – no doubt giving both Lysander and Helena a bit of a fright – and moves seamlessly into couplets. In theory, Demetrius' restored desire for Helena should, as Oberon hoped, restore at least one half of the equation. But this love-juice seems to affect tongues as well as eyes, and the sheer excess and obvious artifice of Demetrius' language (he came close to this kind of hack poetry when we saw him in pursuit of Hermia earlier) undoubtedly helps confirm Helena in her view that both young men are simply bent on ridiculing her.

To look ahead for a moment: this speech, like others of these young lovers, is not dissimilar from what we will hear from Pyramus and Thisbe later (V.i.320–7, for example), though these young courtiers might later choose to ignore that.

Helena, too, continues in couplets, and her opening words are in something of the same heightened tone as Demetrius'. But, rather like Hermia's speech earlier, at lines 155–6 the rhyming couplets are first briefly adjusted by the half-rhyme of 'Hermia' with 'Helena', and those following allow the actor to move through the ending of the lines, barely touching the rhyme, to drive home the individually 'felt' situation in which she finds herself. The young men, however, still charmed, are confined to the strict rhyme scheme and end-stopped lines.

Enter Hermia

176–191 Hermia's arrival, heralded by Demetrius' emphasising '*thy* love', '*thy* dear' to Lysander, brings the promise of yet more confusion and the chance of things falling out preposterously: no doubt Puck can hardly contain himself. Still wandering, lost in the 'Dark night', Hermia has been guided to this spot by the same noisy exchanges we've just been listening to. Now finding alive the man she had thought was dead, her lines could easily run on straight from II.ii.151–62. They underline the radical change in Lysander that she now encounters, as he shifts the focus of his affection from one woman to the other, reflected in the tone of voice he takes to each – cajoling and 'poetic' to Helena, blunt and prosaic to Hermia.

192–4 Hermia can't believe he means it, and neither, for different reasons, can Helena, who now sees it as a plot involving all three of them. And while she might, with difficulty, believe it of the men, she cannot believe that Hermia would be so cruel.

195–219 As she turns specifically to address Hermia, Helena drops out of rhyme and into blank verse as the scene and the quarrel get more serious: some home truths need airing. The change in verse form also means the speech reduces in speed (one of the effects of rhyme is to keep things going) but gains in intensity, as the scene now focuses on the two young women, and Lysander and Demetrius take a back seat. Likening herself to an animal tied to a stake and baited for 'sport' (a popular Elizabethan entertainment), the burden of Helena's complaint is that Hermia has failed to remember how close they were as girls: her phrase 'artificial gods' means 'gods of artifice', picturing them as twin creators, but the echo of 'artificial' is also present in her recollection of that closeness. A modern audience (perhaps having decided Helena is given to slightly over-egging the emotional pudding) may find her image of the two of them 'warbling' a song together, 'both in one key', as a comic one (and I've seen it played to encourage that, as if basic tunefulness were itself something of an achievement). But Helena is reminding Hermia of the harmony that existed in their relationship. The images come thick and fast and are for the most part perfectly easy to take on, but as we've noticed before, there are also moments when Helena seems unable to prevent herself from looking for a more complex image. Here, for example, lines 212 to 214 – a rather complex reference to heraldic divisions on an equally divided, or 'parted', shield, the image possibly prompted by 'parted' and 'partition' (lines 209–10) – may best be cut in a modern performance. Lines which leave an audience none the wiser do little more than create a vacuum in the theatre, and the actor, while she may have worked out what the lines mean and be able to put them into her own words, still has to *say* Shakespeare's lines.

While we realise that youthful friendships, however intense, will (like those with one's parents) be revised, even replaced, as one becomes an adult, and even though there may be a whiff of nostalgia in Helena's speech that embellishes her memories a bit, we can sympathise with her argument that none of that should lead one friend to scorn another. (The relationship between Helena and Hermia, with its echoes of the closeness experienced by Titania and the mother of the Indian boy, has been of particular interest to critics).

220–44   Helena's words are indeed 'passionate', and Hermia's simple and restrained response seems to suggest she is both dismayed at – and hurt by – these accusations. So Helena presents her with the evidence: the radical changes in the two men's attitudes can only be explained by their all being conspirators in a trick, a trick that Hermia has instigated. The thought seems to plunge Helena into the well of self-pity that we've seen she is always close to toppling down into. To Hermia's repeated expressions of bewilderment, Helena catalogues the signs of their pretence: counterfeiting sad expressions, pulling faces behind her back, giving each other sly looks. Are these generalised statements, or has she indeed noticed something? Before she started speaking Lysander and Demetrius were pretty fired up. What have they been doing throughout Helena's speech? Does she misinterpret whatever it is as being directed at her? Whatever, Helena shows herself to be no slouch in finding a theatrical flourish, predicting 'death or absence' will get her out of their hair.

245–65   Lysander's rather florid plea to Helena to stay and hear his excuse brings a gentle rebuke from Hermia, a rather more forceful one from Demetrius: they clearly believe Lysander is still feigning love for Helena, prompting him to assert the truth of his feelings with even greater conviction. Lysander's words prompt a challenge from Demetrius, which Lysander rebuts. (Demetrius' word 'withdraw', which essentially means 'let's go off somewhere and fight', in performances sometimes signals a moment for the two young men to draw their swords, but that may hinder them in the imminent action.) The previously regular verse form is now fragmented as the dialogue flies between the four of them. The vigour of the language is matched by increasingly lively physical action. Lysander plays most of this section with Hermia attached to him like 'a burr', she still calling him 'sweet love' while he tries to shake her off, physically ('like a serpent', echoing Hermia's dream in II.ii and her description of Demetrius earlier in this scene) and with insults – mainly about her dark colouring – and laced with that favourite word of his: hate. Demetrius, for his part, is now addressing Lysander as 'sir', a much cooler term than we've heard before from these youthful contemporaries.

266–82 Demetrius puns on two meanings of the word 'bond': a binding agreement (as in *The Merchant of Venice*) and a form of restraint, the latter here referring to Hermia's hold on Lysander. It seems Demetrius thinks Lysander is using Hermia's clutches ('weak bond') as an excuse not to be able to leave and fight the duel that Lysander challenged him to. Hermia perhaps releases him as she hears what he says in lines 269–70, and then realises – for the first time – that maybe he is not pretending, but has genuinely transferred his love to Helena. But unable to believe that Lysander can truly hate her, and still calling him 'my love', she reminds him – and us – of the incredible speed with which these relationships have shifted, how within the space of one night they appear to have become different people. Indeed, it is only beginning to dawn on her that he left her alone in the forest 'in earnest'. Her choice of word is significant here: 'earnest' is invariable paired in Elizabethan plays with 'game' or, as it is here in line 280, with 'jest', and refers to actual life, not the representation of it in a play. In other words, she is only now confronting the fact that Lysander, for all his earlier vows, might really have transferred his affections to Helena, something he is only too quick to confirm in the most absolute terms.

282–98 It is this exchange that prompts Hermia to turn her attention to Helena. Gone are attempts to mollify Helena – whose

'Fine i'faith' indicates she thinks the game has now entered another phase – with Hermia not only pretending that Lysander does indeed love Helena, but that Helena has deliberately and cunningly (a 'juggler' is a trickster or a wanton person) stolen him from her. Helena, while trying to hold the moral high ground, will get a laugh as her 'gentle tongue' utters a sharp insult to her smaller adversary: 'puppet'. If we didn't already know Hermia might be sensitive to the height difference between them, we do now, as Helena, from that same long acquaintance she articulated so eloquently moments before, knows exactly how to rile her friend, and as they square up to each other the difference in their size will be particularly evident. Hermia works herself into a frenzy of rage (her phrase 'painted maypole' embraces not only Helena's height, but the sexual licentiousness associated with too much make-up and mayday customs); but words alone cannot express her fury, and she launches herself at Helena.

299–317 Calling on the two young men for help – who probably step between the women, or struggle to hold Hermia back – Helena pretends to be (or is?) afraid of Hermia, claiming to be too gentle to retaliate, physically or verbally, though taking care to push the height button again and so provoke Hermia still further. Adopting a tone of one more sinned against than sinning, she first confesses that it was she who told Demetrius of their flight from Athens and into the wood, and now wishes no more than to depart, sad, but in peace.

318–38 The scene seems to be subsiding a little, but it ignites and flares up again as the two men vie for who will defend Helena from Hermia, while Helena (with the youths providing a defensive wall; perhaps Lysander is holding Hermia back) takes another opportunity for more jibes about her height and temper. As an enraged Hermia tries to get past the men to Helena, Lysander stops her with a tirade of his own. Demetrius jealously takes further exception to Lysander appointing himself Helena's protector and showing her any affection. But the time for words is past and, drawing their swords, they stride off to find a place to settle their differences, jostling for who will lead the way and who will follow.

339–44 Left alone with the incensed Hermia, no men to defend her, Helena tries to leave, but Hermia moves to block her exit. (Her phrase 'go not back' may mean 'back to Athens', the sense it has in line 315, but on the Elizabethan stage it may also more specifically refer to the actor's move back upstage to one of the doorways in the tiring-house wall.) They start using rhyming couplets, revving up the scene again, and Hermia's line is threatening enough to suggest a fight might be the women's way, too, of settling their differences. But Helena, slightly delaying her move, puts her longer legs to practical use and suddenly runs off, leaving Hermia stunned, before she too exits.

345–73   The calm after the storm. Blank verse replaces the couplets. As the audience applaud, the actors left on stage may not be in any great hurry to move on. The extreme physical and verbal activity of the previous bit of the scene will have left the audience needing a breather. Oberon seems (a bit late in the day) to be coming to the realisation that Puck may prefer it when things go wrong, indeed may deliberately make them do so. But as Puck points out, he did exactly as he was told by Oberon, who he calls 'King of shadows', Shakespeare's word for actors and a reminder of Oberon's role as the play's 'internal dramatist' (Montrose 1996, p. 107). As Puck gains in confidence, he slips into couplets again. Oberon, also now in rhymed lines that drive the speech on, as if he's thinking on his feet, devises ways for Puck to keep the men from hurting themselves – make it foggy, impersonate their voices to confuse them – then, when they're worn out and sleep, instructs him to put *this* (he's got it with him, or can magically produce it) new potion in *Lysander's* (he stresses the word) eye. The upshot will be that they'll all forget what's happened and be firm friends forever. Of course, our experience of Puck's success in (or even wish to) sort things out may make us think that further confusions lie ahead. Or we might think that that particular plot strand has been played out and that some resolution is needed, dramatically and theatrically.

374–77   Oberon, meanwhile, draws us back to the Titania-Bottom plot. His sequence of actions is significant. He will first 'beg' Titania to let him have the Indian boy (not demand – does this signal a new mood on his part?) and then (but with the implication that only if she agrees to his terms) he will apply the same potion to Titania's eyes, release her from her infatuation with the ass, and order will be restored.

378–88   Puck's image of the approaching dawn is both arresting and macabre, reminding us that while we have no doubted laughed at the comical antics of the lovers, darker forces are also present in this wood, just as they are also a part of love. I noted earlier how Shakespeare is careful to portray the fairies' interventions in the lives of the mortals as essentially benevolent (recall Titania's sympathy for the misery her quarrel with Oberon has inflicted on the lives of the country people, for example) and here Oberon quite explicitly underlines how they differ from those malevolent spirits that are the agents of superstition, witchcraft and fear: 'But we are spirits of another sort' (line 388). Indeed, some critics have suggested that Oberon, rather than Puck, should speak lines 386–7, as being more in keeping with his character and leading into his speech that underlines how he and Puck can – unlike the more sinister spirits, associated with the dark and the past – stay until the dawn has risen, and who are thus associated with light, creation and the future.

389–95   Oberon's description of the dawn is of a very different kind from Puck's, with its striking images of the sun rising like fire in the east, casting its beams on the sea to turn its green to gold. The metre of his lines, with their drive towards the completed transformation of the sea ('Turns' is the simple but enforcing verb), embodies his power and authority. Oberon is plainly associating himself with light, not darkness, but the meaning of his arresting line 'I with the Morning's love have oft made sport' is not immediately clear. This is the fifth time in the play Shakespeare has used the word 'sport', employing it so far to refer to the mechanicals' rehearsal (III.ii.14) and to the amusement that Helena assumes the others are getting from her misfortune. Oberon's reference to the forester in the next line may suggest he means he has gone hunting with the huntsman Cephalus, who was loved by the goddess of the dawn, Eos (Aurora in Roman mythology), and hence the 'morning's love'. (Bottom will later, V.i.196, make a garbled reference to 'Shafalus', which might suggest the story was in Shakespeare's mind as he wrote.) But it has also been suggested that Oberon uses 'sport' here to mean not just having a good time but to refer to some kind of sexual activity (Shakespeare uses the phrase 'act of sport' in *Othello*, for example, to mean sexual intercourse) of his own with Morning, allowing Shakespeare to enforce as strongly as possible Oberon's intimate association with light. No exit is indicated for Oberon in the early copies, but he generally leaves the stage at this point, his closing couplet picking up the pace, encouraging Puck to get on with the plan, not waiting for a reply, and presumably headed for Titania's bower.

396–400   Rebuked by Oberon or not, Puck (calling himself Goblin as if to underline his mischievous side) clearly intends to have his fun with the lovers. His rhyming lines might act as the spell by which he raises the fog, into which Lysander, with his sword drawn, now stumbles.

401–30   This section of the scene offers the actors considerable opportunities to display physical and vocal virtuosity. The lovers will already have had to imitate behaviour in a wood in the dark. Now they must vary that to represent the fog. Scenes set in fog or mist were not common, but were by no means unknown on the Elizabethan stage and might have included the use of smoke (and modern productions often do the equivalent), but generally (and again counter to the theatrical ambitions of Quince & Co.), fog would be conjured up by the actors' gestural and vocal performances. Puck's disorientation of the youths would probably have involved the two rear doors of the stage, and the size of the outdoor stage, plus the two large pillars supporting the cover over the stage, would have offered opportunities for leading them on (see Chapter 1). The large stage also permitted swift movement, and Lysander's references to how 'fast' they're moving, and Demetrius' to his opponent running, never stopping to stand and face him, indicate the speed of the action which, added to all the energy they've already expended in the scene, leads them both in turn to lie down and sleep.

431–47   Helena enters, expressing some pretty conventional images of the night (again to be echoed later by Pyramus), and speaking alternately rhymed lines, shifting from the couplets spoken by the young men that kept the action moving. She, too, sleeps, and as Puck watches and waits for the fourth to arrive, Hermia enters, emotionally and physically much the worse for wear but still with Lysander's safety uppermost in her thoughts. Her lines give the actor very clear instructions what she has to do: show she's weary, stop crawling, decide and show us where 'Here' is, and pray. Exhausted, she sleeps.

448–end of scene   Puck finally gets the antidote into the right person's eye. His epithet for Lysander, 'gentle lover', reminds us that this young man can indeed be such, even though we've seen a rather different side of him in the course of the night. And this simple rhyming charm, calling on the country proverbs, has something of the feel of an ending, of restoring order to confusion.

The Folio stage direction (not in the Quartos) reads 'They sleep all the Act'. What this means is not at all clear. When the play was first performed, outdoors (see Chapter 1), it was common practice to perform plays without breaks, the audience simply going out if they needed to relieve themselves or find refreshment. This practice of uninterrupted performance helps explain the contemporary references to playing times of two hours, which modern audiences, used to performances lasting more like three hours and often with two intervals, find difficult to understand. By the time the Folio was assembled, playing indoors had become much more common, with regular breaks in the action to trim the candles. So it could mean that, outdoors, the lovers remain on stage and are in place as Titania enters or, that they remain on stage during the interval. The latter seems unlikely to me. My own experiments with candle-lit performance in a reconstructed indoor playhouse suggest to me that it would be extremely difficult (and hazardous even by Elizabethan standards) to keep actors prone on stage while the tire-men trimmed the lights and the stage-sitters stretched their legs.

Act IV

Act IV, scene i

0 *Enter* Titania, *and* Bottom *and* Fairies; *and* Oberon *behind them.* Whether or not there has been an interval through which the lovers have remained on stage, they are there at the start of this scene. Counting the lovers, Titania, Bottom, the three named Fairies who appear, and assuming Oberon has a minimum of three attendants too (though none is referred to), there is now a minimum of 13 characters on stage. The stage direction 'Enter', as well as its obvious meaning, can also specify that characters take their places before the scene proper begins: 'enter on a chair', for example.

1–4 The dialogue indicates that Titania leads Bottom (called Clown in the early texts; see comments on opening of III.i), in his ass head, to the 'flowery bed' (a rather more specific location than a 'bank'). They embrace and, as she kisses his ears and he no doubt brays with pleasure, she begins to decorate his 'sleek, smooth head' with the musk roses that we learned earlier (II.i.252, II.ii.3) decorate her bower. It is a wonderful, bizarre tableau, and unsurprisingly provides one of the most common images of the play found on posters and in paintings. Reading, we will need to keep the strangeness of the stage image in mind at all times.

The stillness of this moment and the gentle and affectionate language are in stark contrast to the physical and vocal pyrotechnics of the previous scene. Is the mood post-coital, or has their contact been limited to some loving and gentle embraces? Critics – and productions – differ as to the precise nature of what has taken place between Titania and Bottom: some find it overtly erotic, others discern a more maternal mood, while others find it a curious blend of both, with Titania treating Bottom as if he were at one and the same time her child (a replacement for the changeling?) and her lover. Behind the image, too, there is an echo of the story of Pasiphae, who under a spell copulated with a bull, and gave birth to the Minotaur (see Nuttall 2000).

Representation of this coupling between woman and ass as an overtly sexual encounter is not the prerogative of the twentieth century. A painting by Henry Fuseli (1785) shows a naked Oberon standing observing Titania, also naked, with the Indian boy between them. Bottom, also naked, lies beside Titania, as if asleep. Between Bottom's open legs, Fuseli has placed the figure of a fairy which, if looked at closely, conceal, or might suggest, his genitals. Similarly, an engraving by G. Rhodes, made in the 1790s, and derived from Fuseli, portrays Bottom as a muscular, near-nude figure, embraced by Titania whose right breast is exposed. They are surrounded by tiny fairies (one of whom, naked, spreads his legs to display his very human male genitals), but also by figures the same size as themselves. One of these faces straight out from the picture, and occupies a dominant position to the left of the image, has her arms positioned in a strange way, but one which may suggest an erect penis. The implication of the scene in both images is inescapable (see Orgel 2003, pp. 85–111).

5–26 Bottom has become fully assimilated into the fairy, woodland world. Titania, completely attentive to his needs and desires, has made good her promise that he should be well looked after. While Titania caresses him, Peaseblossom scratches Bottom's head and Cobweb is sent on a mission to bring him honey (though there is actually no exit indicated in the early texts). There is a nice piece of visual comedy as Bottom tries to stop Mustardseed from repeatedly bowing to him and join Peaseblossom in the scratching.

27–38 To entertain him, Titania offers music. Bottom's choice is for 'tongs and bones', a combination of one piece of metal struck by another (as in the 'tongue' of a bell) and clappers of wood, rattled together. My father used to entertain us at home by playing the spoons, clacking them on his knees and elbows as he sang, and this sounds rather similar. Titania's firm interjection – 'Or' – is sometimes taken to mean that she moves immediately to steer Bottom towards food as an alternative to this simple rustic choice, but the F1 stage direction, 'Music Tongs, Rural Music', suggests that, at times anyway, such music played as a background. And there are other appetites to be satisfied. Titania offers Bottom a woodland feast of nuts, but his tastes are simple here, too – a truss of hay. In a modern performance, especially if there is a sense that the characters are sexually sated, Titania's offer to send for 'new nuts' for Bottom, may well raise laughter. In Shakespeare's time, 'nut' was used to refer to the glans of the penis, but 'nuts' for 'testicles' is a twentieth century coining. If the audience does laugh, they might do so again on Bottom's line about dried peas (line 36) – maybe thinking there's another bawdy meaning. There isn't, nor was there then, but any good comic actor will get a laugh here if he wants one. Tired out, Bottom has an 'exposition of sleep' come upon him, another instance of his lexical ambition and attempt to match the speech of his superiors: social hierarchies are repeatedly emphasised throughout the play.

39–44 It is now Bottom's turn to sleep. Titania embraces him again and dismisses the fairies. Her words describe her physical actions – gently 'entwisting' her soft body round his rougher ('barky') body. The image she conjures – of the woodbine (bindweed) entwining the honeysuckle, the ivy twisted round the elm – gives us a clear direction for the two actors to be wrapped in each other's embrace.

It would have meant more to an Elizabethan than it does to us. In a very popular book, Geoffrey Whitney's *Choice of Emblems*, which would have been well known to many in Shakespeare's audience, he printed a woodcut emblem of the vine and the elm which, like the stage image/dialogue takes the form of an image/text (this is reprinted in White 1998, p. 138). In that instance it is an image of the mutual support of friendship. Here, with specifically the 'female ivy' and the rougher maleness of the elm, the relationship is gendered; indeed, it has been suggested that Shakespeare substituted ivy for vine given the extra-marital nature of this relationship.

The enringed finger is a common Shakespearean image of coition (see Carroll 1985, pp. 152–5), but whatever went on between Titania and Bottom during III.ii, it happened out of our sight, and some actors choose this moment of physical embrace to underline the sexual nature of this union between fairy and ass. I do not share the view that displays of physical intimacy between the male actors on the Elizabethan stage were invariably supplanted by the language they speak – there's lots of evidence to the contrary. But the point here I think is that while Shakespeare produces an image not necessarily of marital peace, he creates one of two people, attentive to each other, now in relaxed harmony – the first time we've seen that in the play. (It is, of course, an extra-marital relationship – at least on her part. We've no idea whether or not Bottom has a wife or lover, though Michael Hoffman's film provided him with one; see Chapter 5.)

45–62 As Puck enters, Oberon steps forward. Depending on where he's been placed on stage we may have forgotten his presence, though the scene gains in complexity if we have been throughout aware that he, too, has been watching. His description of the sleeping couple as a 'sweet sight' might surprise us – Titania is his wife after all – but, as we heard in Act I, they seem to have had a relaxed view of each other's sexual conquests or emotional entanglements. However, his language now seems more in keeping with Titania's opening jibe that he is 'jealous Oberon': he earlier indicated that he would 'beg' her to give him the boy, but his account of their meeting suggests it was far from conciliatory. In Oberon's version of events he has already argued with and taunted her for doting on Bottom. His view of Bottom as a 'hateful fool' ('hateful' has more of our sense of 'loathsome'), and the emphasis in Oberon's description of the *crown* of flowers with which this ass is garlanded gives a clue to his anger – Titania has disgraced both the flowers and herself in elevating Bottom in this manner. So Oberon has demanded, and – perhaps to assuage him – this time Titania has given him the Indian boy who has been the cause of this particular quarrel between them, and the boy has been taken to Oberon's 'bower' (the word perhaps gaining particular resonance after the events in Titania's bower) in Fairyland.

63–9   Oberon instructs Puck to remove the ass's head. Oberon's lines are rather complex metrically, and it's not immediately apparent why that should be so: 'transformed' is made tri-syllabic, 'Athenian' also, while 'May all to Athens back again repair' is unnecessarily awkward. Perhaps making the lines harder to speak, and so making the actor take his time, is designed to emphasise the magic and significance of the moment. At the same time, both the pun on 'repair' ('return' and 'make good') and the emphasis on the word (the line would make sense without it) may suggest that Oberon believes there will be an opportunity for the mortals to put right any fracture in their relationships.

70–4   Having dealt with Bottom and the lovers (still asleep somewhere on stage, remember), and moving into rhyming couplets, Oberon releases Titania from the spell, using the antidote he identified in II.i.183–4. The herb 'Dian's bud', that has the power to counteract the charm of love-in-idleness is probably Artemesia, its name appropriately alluding to Diana (Artemis), the goddess of the moon, and of chastity, who has watched over the play in her different guises.

75–101   Titania, waking, is shocked by what she sees, but her reaction to the human Bottom himself, revealed as Puck physically removes the property head, is less clear. (Oberon first instructs Puck to remove the head at lines 63–4, but the action is evidently not implemented immediately, again maybe to increase the dramatic moment.) More music – summoned up by Titania (they are now sharing things, underlined by their rhyming lines) – but this is 'soft' music, appropriate to the spell Oberon casts to make sure the five mortals stay sleeping. The music shifts to the rhythm of a dance, and one that will 'rock the ground'. Unless Bottom danced to the tongs and bones, this is the second dance we've seen in the play, and it marks a significant turning point in the action. Oberon earlier declined Titania's invitation to dance with her and her fairies, but now, in line with the Elizabethan notion of a dance as being not only 'love's proper exercise', but also an active, performative image of harmony in marriage, it signals, as Oberon says, the restoration of his and Titania's relationship (line 86) and the harmony of the natural world. As Antinous urges Penelope in Sir John Davies's *Orchestra* (1594):

> Dancing (bright lady) then began to be,
> When the first seeds whereof the world did spring,
> The Fire, Air, Earth and Water did agree,
> By Love's persuasion, Nature's mighty king,
> To leave their first disordered combating;
> And in a dance such measure to observe,
> As all, the world their motion should preserve.

They exit or, in performances where the roles of the fairy king and queen are doubled with their human counterparts, the dance is often the moment at which, departing as Puck warns that morning is really here now, they transform themselves to Theseus and Hippolyta.

101 Horns sound. Enter Theseus with Egeus, Hippolyta, and all his train The music of the dance is perhaps interrupted by the more strident sound of the wind horns, signalling the intrusion of day and the mortals.

102–10 Does Theseus' perfectly appropriate command that one of his attendants should seek out the forester echo Oberon's earlier description of himself as being 'like a forester' (III.ii.390)? A few lines later, the attendant evidently still there, Theseus repeats his instruction, more firmly this time, for his servant to seek out this character. Will the forester appear? Or is there in this some further sense of how the forest is, as we have seen, the place where the spirit and mortal worlds meet and, at their edges, blur into each other? Is Theseus calling our attention to the fact that he is also, in this play, partly the Fairy King too? Whatever, it is a moment in which Shakespeare captures the connections between these two rulers, a connection that is embodied unmistakably, of course, in those performances where one actor plays both roles. Theseus suggests that he and Hippolyta go to the top of the mountain to watch the hunt in the valley below, where his hounds are being released, and hear how their barking (which, in the playhouse of Shakespeare's day and our own, we can no doubt hear in the distance) echoes around them.

111–26 Titania and Oberon may be reconciled, but these two (who we haven't seen since the first scene of the play of course) seem still to be tense with each other. Now, Hippolyta (the captive queen we should remember) takes full opportunity to underline the comparison between this moment and the time she was hunting with Hercules and Cadmus (classical legendary heroes chosen by Shakespeare, it seems, because their names were well known rather than for any particular association) whose Spartan hunting dogs outdid any others for their 'sweetness of cry' (as the Elizabethans termed the barking of a pack of hounds). Theseus' slightly miffed response suggests she has touched a nerve. He claims that his dogs, also bred from Spartan hounds, are matchless for their size and strength, their baying (likened to a set of bells set to produce a range of tones from high to low), never equalled in Crete or anywhere else (though it's been pointed out that hunting dogs really ought not to be 'slow in pursuit', Sutherland and Watts 2000, pp. 145–6). But before their competitive wrangling can develop, Theseus catches sight of the four sleeping lovers.

127–36 Egeus has lost nothing of his suspicion. The way he says each of the young people's names (Helena, interestingly, still being defined by her relationship to her father or mother – we must be careful not to assume Nedar is male – just as Egeus defines his own daughter) will express his attitude to them, while 'wonder' followed by 'together' will leave us in no doubt of his interpretation of the situation. Theseus deflects these suspicions, but then draws Egeus' – and our – attention back to the fact that this is the day when Hermia has to decide whether she will obey her father's wishes or risk the consequences.

137–44 Woken by the offstage horns (I'm not certain why they don't just shake them awake) the lovers 'start up', kneel and, as Lysander, bewildered at what's going on, begins to speak, they are

commanded by Theseus to stand. The stage positioning will be significant here. We have come full circle, with Theseus, flanked by
Egeus and Hippolyta, confronting the four young people; indeed, his
line 'I know you two are rival enemies' could have been spoken in I.i,
around line 111. But as we, though not Theseus, have seen, there have
been momentous changes since these characters were last together.

145–75 Lysander speaks, the fog in his brain slowly clearing, the
fractured verse with its heavy punctuation and sub-clauses capturing his stumbling efforts to understand what's happened. But there
is now no attempt to evade the truth as there was to evade the law,
and he plainly confesses what he and Hermia planned to do. Egeus,
of course, has been through no transforming experience, and he hits
exactly the same tone and target as in the opening scene. He now
wants Lysander's head, while his indignant repetition of 'my con-
sent', that fully expresses his real concern, is rendered foolish in comparison with Lysander's halting simplicity of expression. Demetrius
is changed, too. He has grown up, and we hear it in his direct,
straightforward words. Not only does he realise that 'gauds' are not
witchcraft, but he freely confesses that he was, indeed, betrothed to
Helena before he took a fancy to Hermia. (We can imagine Egeus'
response to this news; in scene one Lysander used the rather broader
accusation that Demetrius 'made love' to Helena.) Quite how
Hermia responds to being compared to an 'idle gaud' is something
the actress will need to consider; but both young women are silent
during these exchanges. The last two lines of Demetrius' speech,
however, can leave us in no doubt of his sincerity, and Theseus
comes to a decision.

176–85 In the opening scene, Theseus claimed he could not 'exten-
uate' (mitigate) the laws of Athens (I.i.120). Now, recognising that
'some power' (line 164) has restored Demetrius to his 'natural taste'
(line 173), and that he now fully acknowledges his commitment to
Helena, Theseus decides to 'overbear' Egeus, and puts any hope of his
mind being changed beyond discussion by announcing that these
two couples will be married alongside him and Hippolyta. Since
the lovers awoke, Hippolyta has, as she did for most of the opening
scene, remained silent. She and Theseus have had no chance to settle
their spat about (ostensibly) the hounds, but whereas in scene one

Theseus sided with Egeus against the lovers, here he has done completely the opposite. Does she signal approval in some way? Could that be in the way she reacts to Theseus' 'Come, my Hippolyta', with its echo of line 122 in the opening scene? Does he make it a request, or command? As the last line in a speech of completely regular iambic pentameters, the fact that it is a half-line stands out – five beats remain, to be filled with her decision on how to respond.

186–98   Left alone on stage, the lovers share their sense of what's happened, of 'These things' they've experienced, using each other's evidence to try to piece things together, to rationalise their experiences. Shakespeare catches brilliantly their slowly emerging awareness that things are different, the fine line between waking and dreaming: the fact that things can be, as Helena says of Demetrius, both certain and doubtful at the same time.

Although we don't at this point in performance know it, Hermia and Helena will not speak again in the play after this scene (see Chapter 6 for critical responses that focus on the gender/power aspects of the play and male control of unruly females): it is worth noting here, therefore, that Hermia's last words are 'Yea, and my father'.

199–end of scene   The stage has been full and busy throughout the scene, and with the lovers' departure we may think the scene is at an end. But we have forgotten Bottom, who now emerges from wherever on stage he has been sleeping. As has happened before in the play, a waking character reverts, initially, to the moment in the play before he or she was in some way altered, a device that allows Shakespeare to underline the changes that they have undergone. Here, Bottom could be following on from III.i.80 when he went off to wait for his cue from Thisbe to enter. Like the lovers, but with no one with whom to test his memory, Bottom is struggling to come to terms with what's happened. Granville Barker considered this soliloquy of Bottom's to be very inferior stuff, but that is surely a rare misjudgement on Barker's part. In performance we will be aware by this point of the play's strategy of balancing the experiences of different groups of characters – lovers (old and young), fairies and working men. The stage is often full of characters and actions, but there are also moments such as this (another would be where Bottom finds himself abandoned and frightened in III.i), when Shakespeare focuses our attention on an intense individual experience. Our intimate insight into Bottom's attempts to come to terms with events means we will from this point have a more complex understanding of the character, of his inner life.

The speech offers Bottom a route from donkey back to man. 'Heigh ho' may be an opportunity for an echo of his braying, while the actor no doubt can express the lack of velvety ears and a hairy face. Some actors use 'methought I had' to look to see if they still sport a donkey-sized penis. As if Quince's note to Flute/Thisbe that Bottom/ Pyramus has gone to 'see a noise' is still in his ears, or perhaps to underline how confused his senses are, Bottom famously misquotes a famous passage from the bible, Corinthians 2:9 Although his words serve to remind us how untrustworthy our senses are – a core theme of the play – for an Elizabethan audience the lines might have carried further political resonance: behind 'the comic garbling of the allusion and its farcical dramatic context' an 'opposition between sacred and profane knowledge is displaced into an opposition between Bottom's capacity to apprehend the story of the night and Theseus's incapacity to comprehend it' (Montrose 1995, p. 84).

Committed actor that he is, and to confirm the experience he has had, Bottom determines that Quince should write him a 'ballet', for the end of the play. Modern editors invariably emend this to read 'ballad', but in Shakespeare's day 'ballet' could refer to a song to be danced to, or a dance accompanied by singing. Elizabethan plays, serious and comic, were concluded with a jig – a bawdy song and dance, and it's possible that Bottom's 'ballet' suggests he has something similar in mind to perform at 'the latter end' of the play. Bottom's ballet, however, will be dignified by being sung (however inappropriate its subject matter) to accompany Thisbe's death. It will be interesting to hear what the other actors think about that idea.

Act IV, scene ii

0 *Enter* Quince, Flute, Snout and Starveling   We returned to the world of the court in the previous scene, but with Theseus and Hippolyta and their attendants making their way to the wood. We are now back in Athens, later the same day, in Quince's workshop presumably, where we first encountered the workmen (or the 'rabble', as the early texts' stage directions term them).

1–14 Quince's opening question might suggest that Starveling enters separately from the others, having been on an errand to try to locate Bottom. No sign. The play can't go ahead without the leading actor. Unlike the lovers in the previous scene, no one (unless they've had this conversation already) mentions what they saw in the wood before they ran away. Throughout this scene, in the Quarto and Folio editions, Flute is designated as Thisbe in the speech headings. This might just be an error, or does it suggest that Flute is already costumed, or at least taking on some of the characteristics, of the character he will play? A marker of his growing confidence may also be seen as he corrects Quince's description of Bottom as a 'paramour' (though as that word means one who serves royalty or aristocracy as a lover, or the sexual partner of someone who already has a husband or wife, Quince speaks more accurately than he – or any of his companions – knows).

15–22 Snug arrives. Still no news of Bottom, but he's heard that the wedding is to be an even bigger affair than they first thought. If we ever wondered exactly how his fellow actors feel about Bottom, Flute's clearly deeply felt regret that Bottom will miss out on the chance to impress and, perhaps more important to these working men, be financially rewarded by Theseus (sixpence a day would have been a princely sum), will confirm the affection in which he's held. It is a quiet, subdued group who ponder what might have been.

23–end of scene Bottom's entrance into the scene makes almost as big an impact on his fellows as he did with the ass's head on. As they gather round him, eager to hear his tale, he cannot bring himself – or find the words – to tell them. What he *can* do is galvanise them into action. The Duke has dined (which sets the scene in late afternoon; Elizabethans ate supper around 5.30 p.m.), the time for entertainment has come, and their play has been chosen! There are a few last minute things to be done – to check the strings on the beards (Bottom is keen on beards we know from before) and get the right footwear for a comedy (though their play is ostensibly a tragedy), make sure the costumes are clean and their breath sweet.

Act V

Act V, scene i

0 *Enter* **Theseus, Hippolyta, Philostrate, [***with Lords and*
Attendants]**   With the opening of the last scene in Theseus' palace,
the play has come full circle (though of course if we haven't seen the
play before we won't necessarily know it *is* the last scene). The stage
direction mirrors the beginning of the play, and repeated images
such as this provide the opportunity for any changes in relationships or situations to be underlined.

1–27   From the start of the play, and at subsequent moments, the
relationship between Hippolyta and Theseus has seemed strained
and fractious. Now, her first words in this scene – 'my Theseus' –
strike a very different tone ('another key') from when we last saw
them wrangling over whose hounds made the best noise. She sees
the stories the lovers have told (presumably over dinner) as strange,
but Theseus is much more sceptical and dismissive. To him, they
may be strange, but they are certainly no truer than old wives' tales
or stories about fairies ('anticke' – the Q2 and F spelling – carries the
meanings of 'ancient' *and* 'bizarre' or 'fantastic'). But in the sixteenth
century 'toys' also meant 'tricks', so Theseus who, unlike the audience, has not seen any fairies in the play, speaks truer than he knows.
Ironically, too, he is also proclaiming his disbelief in the world of
ancient legends of which he and Hippolyta are a part (Taylor 2003).
    Theseus himself has learned some lessons: he now approves of
the love relationships of the young Athenians, but his ideas about
the relative values of reason and imagination remain fundamentally
unchanged. He believes the lovers' stories are the product of their
over-fertile imaginations, a tendency, he argues, shared by lunatics
(who, under the moon's influence, are given to seeing visions), lovers
(who find beauty where right-minded people do not, or are attracted
to others for no apparent rational reasons) and poets (here, as was
common in Shakespeare's day, meaning playwrights) whose pens, in
a frenzy of inspiration, give form to their imaginations in the things
they create on stage. And it is this power of imagination that creates
realities from fantasy, just as Theseus suggests we might (again he
speaks unwittingly), in the dark forest, suppose a bush to be a bear,

all such things being – to him – merely insubstantial fantasy. This is his longest speech in the play, and the only one in which he, or his own situation, is not the subject. Does it stand apart, self-contained and akin to an aria that develops a theme beyond the immediate concerns of the dramatic moment, or is its purpose in part to start to draw together different strands of the ideas that have run through the play on imagination and representation? One thing is certain, this is Theseus speaking, not Shakespeare, and it is within the context of the events of this play that we must interpret it.

Hippolyta, however, is not to be moved from her own view. She considers that the fact that the lovers are 'transfigured' – *all* agree about what happened in the wood, and the ways in which they've *all* changed – suggests that there's more to what they recount than mere fiction. Whatever happened to the lovers, she argues, it has produced in them something of great 'constancy', the word suggesting not just the truth of their account, but fidelity in the relationships of these young people on the brink of marriage, and quite the opposite of the random 'doting' that earlier dominated their thoughts and actions.

Enter the lovers

28–38 Their appearance (very different from the tired and dishevelled group we saw in the previous scene) and attitudes of happy friendship may well confirm Hippolyta's view. Theseus' welcome is fulsome to say the least; has he been swayed by Hippolyta's words? As at the play's opening, lovers are still waiting for time to pass before they can consummate their relationships (Lysander's and Theseus' references to 'bed' and 'bed-time' make it quite clear what they, at least, are waiting for; the women remain silent). For Theseus it may be three hours rather than the four days he saw stretch before him at the start of the play, but that still leaves a 'long age' and 'torturing hour' to get through.

In the Quartos, Egeus is missing from this scene. The Folio includes him but excludes Philostrate, with the lines spoken by Philostrate assigned to Egeus. However, although Philostrate doesn't speak in I.i (simply responding to Theseus' command to go and fix up some entertainment) the fact that he is identified in that scene and in this one in the Quartos, might suggest that it should be Egeus, the character who doesn't acknowledge change in others, or change himself, who is excluded from this scene. Or would a performance choose to have him there, present – but meaningfully silent – like Hippolyta in scene one? In his early comedies, Shakespeare is willing to allow those who have sought to obstruct true love to be absorbed into the play's finale, while in his later plays (As You Like It, Twelfth Night, for example) he takes a tougher line, excluding such characters from the happy resolution. I believe he may be doing the same thing here.

38–60 Philostrate, as Master of the Revels, presents Theseus with a list of entertainments from which to select one. Although it isn't clear where he heard it from, Bottom earlier claimed their play of *Pyramus and Thisbe* was 'preferred', which he, his fellows (and, probably, we too), took to mean that it was chosen for performance. Shakespeare may have forgotten that, or perhaps Bottom didn't realise that they'd only been short-listed at that point. In most modern editions, Theseus reads out the possible choices, whereas in the Folio, it is Lysander who reads out each brief description and Theseus who comments and selects. This allocation of lines is theatrically effective, and may reflect the division employed in early performances and noted in the prompt copy (as well as following, perhaps, the practice of Shakespeare's company). Lysander's involvement also underlines how he – unlike his (here) absent father-in-law – is now fully absorbed into the court. Some productions have chosen to let Philostrate read out the contenders, gaining some fun from his reactions to Theseus' responses.

Theseus declines the first play, not simply perhaps because a combination of harp and eunuch doesn't appeal, or because of the unsuitably violent theme, but maybe also because Hercules rather outshines him as a hero, and maybe he thinks it might rekindle his earlier rivalry with Hippolyta. The subject matter of the second play might equally not be appropriate for a wedding (though Theseus takes the chance to remind everyone of his military conquests) and the third, with its evidently serious and satirical message (Pennington imagines it as an Elizabethan agit-prop play; 2005, 165–6) clearly strikes Theseus as not the thing for a celebration. That just leaves *Pyramus and Thisbe* which, with its apparently contradictory elements, clearly intrigues him.

61–84   Philostrate's description of *Pyramus* is bewildering, and he's presumably exaggerating for comic effect or to disparage it. Whatever, his comments on it – his inability to take it seriously (especially the sad bits) – and on the intellectual limitations of its performers, contribute to establishing the attitude of the onstage characters to the play they're about to see. We, who have shared with Quince and his crew their committed, if sometimes artistically naïve, preparations, may for our part be taking something of an attitude to Philostrate.

Theseus is determined to hear it (one of the references to 'hearing' rather than 'seeing' a play, references that are, in fact, not as common as is often thought), despite Philostrate's efforts to dissuade him. Philostrate even claims to have seen a rehearsal, though when that would have been is not immediately obvious. In his judgement the play is valueless: over-written and over-acted, only worth seeing to make fun of the performances. More to the point, its actors are 'hard-handed men', who never used their brains until now. In his disdain for these artisans he sounds like Puck when he came across the 'hempen homespuns' in the wood. In comparison to Philostrate's superior tones, Theseus' generous response may partly suggest why he is impressed by the 'simpleness and duty' expressed by Lysander and Demetrius in their explanations of the events in the wood.

Theseus instructs Philostrate to summon the actors, and invites the women to take their places. Does this mean that the men (other than Theseus who presumably has some chair of state) do not sit, or just that it's 'ladies first'?

The staging of this scene (as so often with plays-within-plays) can be problematic, especially where to position the onstage audience and the players. In Chapter 1 I discuss possible solutions in the original playhouse, and in Chapter 4 consider the staging used by Beerbohm-Tree, whose solution is typical of end-staging. The issue is that we, and the onstage audience, have to be able to see Pyramus and Thisbe while the court characters need to be able to speak to each other and to us.

85–105   Hippolyta, perhaps hesitating to take a seat, delays the start of the performance, though her admission that she finds no pleasure in seeing people struggle beyond their abilities is more generous than Philostrate's dismissal of the mechanicals' ambitions. Theseus, speaking particularly gently, tries to reassure her that all that is needed is that they should take the performance for what it is and respond to the actors' efforts generously. Line 92 is short, and may suggest that, as Hippolyta does not answer, Theseus pauses while he looks for a specific example to make his point clearer. Drawing on his own experience (and possibly alluding to instances involving Queen Elizabeth; see Montrose 1995, pp. 80–1), he once again stresses how the thing he most values and respects is the intention that motivates someone to speak, not how elaborate his or her language might be.

106–7 Philostrate interrupts this conversation to announce the prologue, and Hippolyta and Theseus take their seats. We know that the play will tell a love story that ends in disaster. But will the performance end in the same way?

108–25 Quince enters to a trumpet fanfare.

The famous De Witt drawing of the Swan playhouse shows a figure with a trumpet up in the roof, and Shakespeare's contemporary, Thomas Dekker, wrote of the Prologue giving 'the trumpets their cue that he's upon point to enter'. In addition to meaning 'ready', the word 'addressed' that Philostrate uses to describe Quince could carry also the sense of being 'made ready with the proper clothing or costume' (OED). What this might be is unclear. In only a few instances in contemporary plays is any indication given of how the Prologue (or Chorus as the figure is also termed) was costumed: in 'black cloaks' (Four Prentices of London), 'like Fame' (The Travels of Three English Brothers) or 'by an Amazon with a battle-axe in her hand' (Landgartha), for example. (The idea of Quince as an Amazon is a tempting one, but given their fear of the offence a lion might give, the chance of offending Hippolyta would have certainly been too great.) In Richard Brome's later comedy, A Jovial Crew, the prologue is spoken by 'the poet', or playwright, himself, though again how that figure was dressed, if in other than his normal clothes, is not known.

The unfamiliar setting, the sudden realisation that there's an audience (and a rather important one) and the perhaps unexpected flourish of trumpets, conspire to put Quince off. We probably won't recall from III.i that the prologue was to be written in 'eight and six' or 'eight and eight' (and the terms wouldn't mean much to a modern audience anyway), but Quince has in fact chosen two quatrains concluding in a couplet.

Bottom earlier proposed (III.i.15–20) that the prologue should focus only on him and his role, but Quince has decided otherwise, using it as an opportunity first to engage with their audience. Just like the 'great clerks' Theseus referred to, Quince makes 'periods in the midst of his sentences' and forgets his 'practised accents' (learned lines). While he waits for his cast to join him (his performance can't have helped their own nerves backstage), he is subjected to the onstage audience's unflattering comments on his delivery, led by Theseus, who seems instantly to have forgotten what he's just said to Hippolyta about being generous in their response to the play.

The courtiers display precisely the kind of behaviour that Ben Jonson parodies in his presentation of those who sat on the stage at the indoor playhouses; see The Magnetic Lady, for example. So far as we know, no audience members ever sat actually on the stage of a public playhouse, and their presence here, in this scene, is clearly a staging of the arrangement found at court. In other words, their position and dialogue identify their social status.

125–50   The cast enter, again heralded by a flourish. (The Folio, following the prompt copy, names the trumpeter as one Tawyer, a trace of an early performance.) We've never seen them in their costumes before, and Quince's opening suggestion that we might 'wonder at this show' will probably accurately sum up our response. The word 'show' might indicate that the actors take up position in a tableau and then perform some kind of dumb show to match the prologue, a common staging practice in the period. This would give us time to absorb and enjoy the costumes – especially the actual solutions they have come up with to the knotty staging issues we saw them confront in rehearsal – before the play proper begins.

Quince, however, seems to have recovered a bit, and this second prologue is much better, setting out plot and characters clearly and concisely. Speaking confidently, Quince first introduces Pyramus, followed by Thisbe (Quince stressing the second syllable of 'certain' to comic effect but undoubtedly and pointedly pronouncing 'Ninus' correctly), then Wall, played by Snout, covered, as planned, with building materials. Starveling, as Moonshine, carries a lantern, a thorn bush, and leads a dog. This was probably a stuffed dog (Henslowe's inventory lists one) or, possibly, a real one, such as was probably used in *The Two Gentlemen of Verona* and which were not uncommon on the music hall stage in the nineteenth and early twentieth centuries.

Shakespeare stays close to the narrative and style of Arthur Golding's version of the *Pyramus and Thisbe* story (see pp. 100–1), but having throughout the play so far demonstrated his own brilliance in finding different styles for different moments, Shakespeare is also clearly mocking – but not I think ridiculing – earlier styles of dramatic writing. A few years earlier, in the first line of the prologue to *Tamburlaine*, Marlowe had set out his manifesto for the new drama, consigning to the past the 'jigging veins of rhyming mother wits' and it's these Shakespeare has in his sights here. In Quince's speech, the repetitions of 'did', archaic words such as 'hight' (called, or named), words inserted to pad out the metre, comic alliteration – are all typical of earlier styles and so contribute to the effect. The actors of this inset play will need to find a style of performance that matches the language, and one that is as different from how they perform as their 'real' characters as this language is from the language those characters speak. The real danger will be to over-act, to send up this play-within-a-play (see Williams 1997, Chapter 4 below, *passim*).

Quince's emphatic repetition in 'there, there to woo' may just be inserted for the metre, but it may also suggest he is indicating some place on stage which will represent Ninus' tomb (possibly the curtained central opening, if there was one). It's not clear either whether we are to imagine the mulberry tree in whose shade (in Ovid/ Golding) the lovers had agreed to tarry, or whether they have provided a property tree (Henslowe lists three in the Admiral's Men's possession) or, as was common, are employing one of the stage pillars (again assuming there were any at the playhouse in question).

151–61   The prologue over, Quince and some of the actors withdraw, leaving Wall on stage. Thinking there's a gap in the action, Theseus and Demetrius joke with each other (might the exiting Bottom hear 'asses', and would he react if he did?), but Wall has his prologue to speak, too. He again calls attention to the signifiers of his costume (though his addition of 'stone' – and there's mention of hair in a moment – might indicate they've rather overdone it). At this time, unlike now, 'sinister' was stressed on the second syllable; doing so makes it easier to rhyme with 'whisper' and will also add comic value. (Evidently, in some productions, Wall has pronounced 'sinister' in the modern way and, seeking his rhyme, followed it with 'whinisper': not recommended.)

162–5 Again, the slight pause while Bottom, as Pyramus, enters is filled with a 'witty' exchange between Theseus and Demetrius, this time complimenting the performance. Their joke hinges on the audience's understanding of 'partition' both as a wall and as the division of a formal discourse, from the Latin 'partitio'. The latter meaning is unlikely to be picked up by a modern audience, so causing the witticism to fall flat, a recurring problem for the actors playing the courtiers in this scene. The two exchanges so far may suggest these two characters are positioned close to each other, but they could as easily (and more effectively for the audience, certainly) be passing these comments across the actors' playing space; there is certainly no reason to suppose that these are in any way expressed in a considerate *sotto voce*.

166–78 Theseus calls for silence as Bottom enters (what beard has he chosen? Is the string secure?). It was common for plays performed in daylight in the open air to establish time of day through language, and the comedy here comes from the excess with which this is pursued, the repetition of words and lines. When Bottom asks Wall to show him his 'chink', most editions insert a stage direction (there is none in the early copies) to the effect that 'Wall parts his fingers', though the Norton edition is less prescriptive, simply noting 'Wall shows his chink'. Certainly, productions have found a whole variety of actions for Snout at this point: 'stones' in Shakespeare's time was a slang term for testicles, and this has suggested to some playing Wall that they might make a chink by standing with their legs apart.

179–84 As Bottom curses the Wall's 'stones' for deceiving him, Theseus once again interrupts the performance, but Bottom, coming right out of character, is on hand to put him right, explaining patiently, rather as one might to a child unaccustomed to play-going, that his line is, in fact, Thisbe's cue. And indeed, right on cue, she comes.

185–200 The comedy with Flute's portrayal of Thisbe is that, unlike the youths who played the female roles, he is not so accomplished. And while they undoubtedly had light, unforced voices, Flute apparently speaks in a strange, high voice. Similarly, there is nothing to suggest that (except when calling attention to the fact that they are male) the professional young actors used anything other than delicate gestures to suggest they were female, whereas Flute is working hard at being feminine (though see my discussion of Tim Supple's production in Chapter 4, and Michael Hoffman's film in Chapter 5).

The joke also depends on Thisbe having been given a series of lines with double meanings – here again playing on the image of her kissing Wall's hairy stones. Her phrase 'knit up in thee' hints at sexual activity ('knit' could mean 'pregnant'), and 'straight way' (line 199), 'come' (line 200) and 'Part discharged' (line 201) obviously do too. The exchange between the lovers through the chink draws its comedy from its clumsy and contrived rhyme. A modern audience will be unlikely to get the mistake of 'Limander' (probably meant to be Leander, or Lysander – the latter would prompt laughter from the onstage audience) or the references to Shafalus and Procrus rather than Cephalus and Procris (both stories of classical tragic lovers). But laugh they will as Quince no doubt rolls his eyes in despair as Bottom mispronounces 'Ninny', and (if 'stones' has determined how the chink is made), Thisbe kisses the Wall's 'hole'. Cheerful vulgarity of this kind was common in moral interludes (look at the anonymous *Mankind* for example), and it is used here for comic contrast with the tragic love story, the 'concord of this discord'.

201–14 The lovers exit, vowing to meet at the tomb, and Wall announces his departure from the play. With the stage empty for a moment, it seems like it's the interval, and the court audience discuss the play. Not everyone is enjoying it. Hippolyta (who earlier expressed her dislike of seeing people out of their depth) is particularly scathing and her comments provoke another disagreement with Theseus. He argues that even the very best actors are only ever pale imitations of the real life person they impersonate, and that a bit of imagination can make even a poor performance tolerable, to which she sourly responds that these players display no imagination at all. But, he responds, if they think they are excellent and we do the same, they can be. What harm lies in that? The appearance of Snug and Starveling, as Lion and Moonshine, halts their wrangling.

215–22 After the lengthy discussions in rehearsal about how to handle the potentially disturbing presence of a lion on stage, we are obviously interested to see how things have worked out. Here, as planned, Snug addresses the ladies, explaining that he is, in fact, just plain Snug, and on no account should be taken for a lion. In performance, it is common for Snug, on announcing his name, to reveal himself as if his audience will be astonished to see a man! This is the second animal mask we have seen. Will some distinction need to be made between how Shakespeare's company and Quince's represent an animal? These men, we must remember, while limited as actors are skilled with their hands, and there's no reason therefore why their properties should be crudely made.

223–54 Before Starveling can pick up his cue, the audience once again intervene with some tortuous jokes about lions, foxes and geese that a modern audience will have difficulty in laughing at, both because they may not find them funny but also because of their rudeness in response to the actors. How seriously now do we take Theseus' claims about his sensitivity in dealing with other people's nervousness?

Starveling has no sooner spoken his first line than they butt in once more. Starveling goes back to the start of his speech, but after just another two lines they interrupt him again. In fact, though Hippolyta claims she's getting bored with this Moon, the audience are speaking more than he is. Performances often cut these interjections from the court (perhaps not wanting the lovers to appear too boorish and so lose sympathy), but though that speeds up the action of the inset play, their removal has significant impact on how we, the theatre audience, receive the whole play at this point and our shifting attitudes to the basic, but well-intentioned skills of the mechanicals and the supercilious indifference of the courtiers. More immediately, it is the obstacles the courtiers' comments put in Starveling's way that provoke him into tetchily condensing his verse speech into his own plain words.

As I have noted in Chapter 6, a good deal of recent criticism has explored the play as, in Richard Wilson's phrase, 'a play about poetry and power' (Dutton 1996, pp. 204–5) in which serious issues lie just beneath the comic surface, such as the truth behind the mechanicals' fears that they may be hanged if they offend with their play. It may be worth noting here, therefore (as my Penguin edition does not) that Starveling's costume reflects an 'ancient and popular superstition' that tells of a 'poor man which stole a bundle of thorns' for firewood and was punished by being 'set into the moon, there for to abide for ever'. When Theseus suggests that 'the man should be put into the lantern' (line 239–40), a 'joke' repeated by Demetrius (line 253), we may need to remember that 'in the lantern' meant to be hanged from the post (Wilson, in Dutton 1996, pp. 210–11).

255–63 With Thisbe's entrance, the scene shifts to Ninny's tomb (as the players stubbornly insist on calling it; Quince must be tearing his hair out with frustration). Quince earlier stressed where this bit of the play might be performed, but the actors' concern about verisimilitude suggests they won't leave the setting to the words alone: in some performances, for example, a tombstone is placed on stage, or Thisbe may even bring a tomb on with her.

This is Snug's big moment, and anxious as he was in rehearsal, he makes the most of it, roaring boldly and playing with the scarf as a cat would with a mouse, before exiting to a round of applause from the court. But perhaps Theseus' word 'moused' suggest Snug's roar is more of a strangulated squeak? In the exchanges a few lines earlier Hippolyta made a sarcastic remark about the moon, for which Theseus, politely but firmly, rebuked her. Here, while the others praise Snug, she finds good things to say about Starveling as Moonshine: maybe his blunt outburst did some good.

264–79 In fact, in some way, the play seems to be winning its audience over. Pyramus enters again, taking four lines (that sound as if they were originally written about the sun) to thank the moon for shining brightly. Seeing the bloodstained scarf dropped by Thisbe as she fled from Lion, Pyramus now moves into something like the 'eight and six' promised by Quince earlier, but with added internal rhymes. Bottom undoubtedly makes the most of his words (including his alliterations) and Quince's thesaurus-inspired last line.

280–2 Despite the excessiveness of the language, and any business Bottom might add, Theseus acknowledges an honesty of feeling in the performance, and even Hippolyta seems moved in some way, despite herself ('beshrew' is the clue here).

283–98 'O wherefore, Nature' shifts the writing back to iambics, before returning to four-and-six for Bottom's death. It has what has become a classic motif of over-acted deaths – the infliction of the fatal wound, but the continued speech of the dying man, here first banishing the moon before he expires with the repetition of 'die', five times. The property sword offers the actor a whole host of comic opportunities, too, and Bottom will undoubtedly take full advantage of them. (We might remember that Bottom promised earlier to grace Thisbe's death with a ballad of his dream; but only Richard Griffiths, in the 1977 RSC production seems to have done so.)

299–307 Again the inset play is interrupted by the interjections of the court (and so again are often cut), as the men pun (pretty impenetrably to a modern audience) on ace/ass, though now Hippolyta seems to be following the action more closely.

308–39 Thisbe's reappearance is the cue for her 'passion', a set speech, often accompanied by appropriate gestures (see White 1998, pp. 69–70). Once the courtiers stop their tortuous word-play and allow Thisbe to begin, her speech continues the joke of inappropriately pairing words and senses that has been a feature of the mechanicals' scenes: here, she describes a dead lover who has 'lily' lips and a 'cherry' nose (more suited to a heroine than hero), with 'yellow' cheeks, and green eyes (associated with jealousy rather than love). Nevertheless, and especially in contrast with the courtiers' crass behaviour (another reason to resist the temptation to cut their lines), there is a sense of genuine feeling in her call to the Fates, some truly striking images, such as 'his thread of silk' – less humdrum than Bottom's own 'thread and thrum' – and in the surprising dignity of her farewell to life. That's not to say there isn't comedy in her death, too: Edward Sharpham's near-contemporary play, *The Fleire* (1607), may reflect the kind of business that accompanied this moment when a character compares something to being 'like Thisbe in the play, 'a has almost killed himself with the scabbard' (II, 434–5, also recalling Ovid's version, see pp. 100–1). Indeed, in this simultaneous moment of death and laughter we experience something typical not only of Shakespeare's own writing but of Elizabethan and Jacobean drama as a whole: the secret is to play both moods with equal conviction.

340–5   Certainly Thisbe seems at last to have silenced the audience's smart-aleck responses; Theseus and Demetrius merely observe that only the inanimate have survived. Flute, at the first rehearsal, was perhaps the most nervous at the casting – uncertain of his masculinity and clearly concerned at the jibes that might be aimed at him in women's clothing. But none of that transpired, and he seems to have in some way risen to the challenge in a particularly striking manner. (See Chapter 4 for specific discussion of this point.) Indeed, Flute may have stolen the acting honours, and Bottom (though the Quartos give the speech to Lion) may be aware of this as he leaps to his feet once more to ensure the audience fully understand the play's outcome, in his excitement once more characteristically mixing up his words.

346–52   Theseus' response is tricky to unpick. Under a veneer of polite praise there seems a vein of the same superiority he and the others displayed throughout, a desire to display his own cleverness rather than offer the generous respect he trumpeted for himself before the play began. There is no mention of any specific reward (certainly no sixpence a day), not even warm thanks: just a rather reserved approval. Theseus and the others in the audience have not come out of this well.

The offer of an epilogue is declined, but the bergomask is requested. All performances in outdoor playhouses, comedies and tragedies, appear to have concluded with a dance, commonly a jig. This was a comic (usually bawdy) song and dance, here performed by two of the mechanicals (possibly including Flute as the theme of the jig may well, in the circumstances, have been relations between a man and woman) with music provided by some or all of the others. In many productions before the 1960s it was common for the dance to be performed somewhat ineptly, as something of a condescending joke at the mechanicals' expense (and so in line with the attitudes expressed by the courtiers to their play). But it is surely an expression of their particular folk culture, brought into and shared with the world of Theseus' court.

353–60   It is not clear exactly when Bottom and the others leave the stage. Performances make different choices, but they usually do so at the end of their dance, before Theseus begins to speak, often on the assumption that he would not speak so disparagingly of their efforts ('This palpable gross play'), were they still present. But that has not held him back so far, and a performance will need to judge the moment in line with how it has played the shifting attitudes of the audience to the mechanicals' efforts and the courtiers' behaviour.

Theseus now moves from prose into verse, and the tone and mood of the scene change accordingly. His reference to 'fairy time' is presumably a joke, as we have already heard him dismiss 'fairy stories' as merely the product of the overactive imaginations of young lovers. It reminds us that though the worlds of the play – of the court, working men and fairies – have come into close contact with each other, and that some have been transformed (or translated or transfigured) by these experiences, some remain hermetically sealed from each other, unaware (as we no longer are) of the power of these forces in their lives. The burst of warm, creative humanity afforded by the mechanicals has gone and the mortals who remain can seem rather cold in comparison. The wedding night is heralded by the 'iron tongue' of midnight; the night itself has a 'heavy gait' rather than the spring in its step that the immediate prospect of wedded love might bring. Even Theseus' command for extended revels has a dry formality about it.

361–80   The courtiers exit and Puck enters, carrying a broom, a symbolic prop from even earlier drama than that which has been sweetly savaged by Shakespeare in the inset play (but see Wall 2001 for a discussion of the 'domestic' imagery implied here). Speaking in alternately rhymed trochaic lines (i.e., lines with a stressed beat, followed by an unstressed, here with seven syllables), he sets an image of a restful, bucolic night against one of a world of real dangers, real lions and wolves howling at a real moon. It reminds us that the wood in which much of the play took place is, especially at night, a place not only of magic but a dangerous and forbidding one too, where, to the ominous call of the owl, ghosts – the 'damnèd spirits' he referred to in III.ii – appear to roam abroad. Here, Diana is configured as Hecate – who ruled in heaven as Cynthia, on earth as Diana and in hell as Hecate – reminding us of the ambivalent sense of illusion and uncertainty contained within the play's moon imagery. Suddenly, however, Puck breaks this sombre mood with the word 'frolic', shifting to couplets, and announcing himself as the 'sweeper in', or herald, of the fairy kingdom.

381–412   The arrival of Oberon and Titania, with all their train, is an echo of their first appearance in the play, but they now present an image of unity, not conflict. Oberon's first speech follows Puck's rhyme scheme, but Titania's is in couplets, and Oberon follows her lead, another instance where the form of the language embodies a relationship. In the 'glimmering light' – perhaps imagined firelight or from tapers carried or even worn by the fairies (as suggested in *The Merry Wives of Windsor*, IV.iv.50) – they both (no silent partners now) instruct the fairies to dance and sing. Then Oberon (possibly speaking with music underscoring his words), blesses the house, the union of the mortal lovers and (drawing on an image of a writer 'blotting' his page) promises protection of any children they will have, who will be physically perfect. However, as throughout the play, for those in the audience who know the story of Hippolytus, Theseus' son, whose physical beauty was his downfall there may be a sombre, ironic undertone to his words (see Nuttall 2000). And while Theseus may, indeed, as he promised at the play's opening, have found a 'different key', Oberon seems completely changed from the vengeful, self-centred being we first encountered. He gives each fairy droplets of dew that he has blessed, and bids them go throughout the palace to anoint the sleepers, and then to meet again with him at daybreak. The vibrant energy of *Pyramus and Thisbe* allows the performance the opportunity to shift gear after the exit of the mortals. But the three sections that conclude the play – Puck with the broom, the dance and song, and Oberon's beautiful benediction – will nevertheless need to be aware that the play needs to move purposefully to its conclusion, and that the more these moments can overlap with each other, the better.

413–end of scene   Puck is left alone on stage. As at the endings of other plays by Shakespeare and plays by other writers, Puck to a degree 'breaks the frame' by directly acknowledging the audience, but he does not come out of character. It seems that it is not just Puck himself, or even the fairies, but all the characters – and the actors themselves – who are 'shadows'. They are all at once both actors and spirits, who wish to avoid the hisses of an audience's harsh criticism, but who are still playing a part, still Puck, still Robin Goodfellow. More profoundly, Puck suggests that in the process of watching a play, an audience, like those in love, has suspended its rational judgement and embraced other worlds as one might in a dream. We as spectators, here, have indeed supposed bushes to be bears and cannot now deny the transforming power of imagination. But the mood at the play's end is a complex one. We will have laughed at the lovers' disarray in the wood and at the performance of *Pyramus and Thisbe* and may welcome the (re)pairings of the human's relationships. But at the same time Shakespeare (as he often does in the comedies he wrote in the next few years), reminds us that we cannot ignore the darker aspects of human experience: that beyond the walls of the (play)house, the serpent's tongue remains sharp, the hungry lion roars and the future may hold unforeseen dangers and disappointments, and that dreams can also be nightmares.

When Thomas Platter, a Swiss who visited London in 1599, attended a performance at the Curtain playhouse, he wrote that 'in conclusion they danced very charmingly in English and Irish fashion'. That doesn't sound much like a jig, or the bergomask at the end of Pyramus and Thisbe. But it does recall the dance of Titania and Oberon, and may suggest that something similar was performed by Theseus/Oberon, Hippolyta/Titania and the other mortals and fairies, a dance perhaps repeated at the end of the whole play, again enforcing the blurred edges of mortal and spirit worlds, of theatre and dream, and the capacity of magic, of performance and imagination to create life shaping and life shifting visions.

3 The Play's Sources and Cultural Context

Samuel Taylor Coleridge described Shakespeare as 'myriad-minded', and it is an apt phrase to describe the range of sources and influences that the playwright drew on for *A Midsummer Night's Dream*. Indeed, the play is unusual – *Love's Labour's Lost* and *The Tempest* are the only other examples – in that Shakespeare used no single source for the main narrative or characters but drew – at times quite extensively, at others with simply a hint or glancing reference – from numerous literary works, contemporary ideas and beliefs, reports of public entertainments and events, his own experience of theatrical practices, the Warwickshire countryside and his knowledge of its folklore. To give a sense of this diversity I have selected elements of the play, and provided brief extracts from appropriate sources, some of which appear to have directly influenced Shakespeare.

Dreams, imagination and perception

> The phantoms of sleep do commonly walk in the great road of natural and animal dreams, wherein the thoughts or actions of the day are acted over and echoed in the night. … Men act in sleep in some conformity unto their wakened senses; and consolations or discouragements may be drawn from dreams which intimately tell us ourselves.
>
> Sir Thomas Browne (1650)

As Barbara Freedman writes, as 'one of our culture's most important theoretical texts on dreaming', *A Midsummer Night's Dream* is itself a prime source for our understanding of 'the Renaissance mind and how it organises experience' (in Kehler 1998, p. 181). The play, however, also draws on a range of earlier and contemporary views on dreams, dreaming and the imagination. The most significant source of classical views on the nature of dreams and of their interpretation was the theoretical and practical study, *Oneirocritica*, by Artemidorus of Daldis, written in the second century AD. Artemidorus sought to create a classification of dreams, basically distinguishing between dreams that offered predictions of future events and those which did not, while recognising that the same dream may have different meanings according to who dreams it. *Oneirocritica* ran to several editions, becoming the model for the dream books that were so popular in sixteenth-century England, and an English translation, itself translated from a French version, appeared in 1606. Thomas Newton's 1577 English translation of Cicero included *The Dream of Scipio*, as well as the influential commentary on it by the fifth century writer Macrobius. Shakespeare might also have known Thomas Hill's *Most Pleasant Art of the Interpretation of Dreams* (1576), in which he wrote that 'a man … doth more comprehend in his dream than waking … because in a dream is more resolved than in the day, which is troubled through the doings of the outward sense' (quoted by Holland 1994, p. 11), literary works such as Chaucer's dream poems or popular pamphlets such as William Lilly's *A Groatsworth of Wit for a Penny*, or *The Interpretation of Dreams*, still widely read a century later. More sceptical views were expressed by writers such as Thomas Nashe, 'the most contemptuous of Renaissance commentators on dream-theories' (Holland 1998, p. 10), who wrote in *The Terrors of the Night*, 1594 (which he dedicated to Elizabeth Carey; see p. 3) that a dream 'is nothing else but a bubbling scum or froth of the fancy, which the day hath left undigested; or an after-feast made of the fragments of idle imaginations'.

It is relevant too that early modern writers on dreams frequently linked them to those seasonal holidays that focused on the seeking of prophetic dreams, particularly Midsummer Eve, which had become associated with 'midsummer madness'. Indeed, the relationship between dreams, imagination and madness, such as Theseus makes (V.i.2–22), remained central to thinking on the subject. As Marjorie Garber explains, it is also from this native tradition that the figures of Puck, Queen Mab (*Romeo and Juliet*) and Ariel (*The Tempest*) emerge 'as inhabitants of Shakespearean dream worlds', worlds which are 'places of metamorphosis, regeneration and renewal and function in the realm of the imagination' (1974, pp. 9, 10). Indeed, as she and others have observed, Hermia's dream (II.ii.151–62) is the only 'real' one in the play.

Document 1

Simon Foreman was born in 1552 and practised as an astrologer and doctor in London from 1583 until his death in 1611. Between 1564 and 1602 he kept a diary in which he recorded three visits to the Globe playhouse, as well as three dreams he had about himself and Queen Elizabeth. The longest of these recollections involves a weaver with a red beard and reveals Foreman's erotic fantasies about the queen.

> Anno 1597 the 23 January: about 3 a.m. I dreamt that I was with the queen, and that she was a little elderly woman in a coarse white petticoat, all unready [partially undressed]. And she and I walked up and down through lanes and closes [courtyards], talking and reasoning of many matters. At last we came over a great close where there were many people and there were two men at hard words [arguing]. And one of them was a weaver, a tall man with a reddish beard, distract of his wits. And she talked to him, and he spake very merrily unto her, and at last did take her and kiss her. So I took her by the arm and pulled her away and told her the fellow was frantic [mad] and so we went from him. And I led her by the arm still and then we went through a dirty lane. And she had a long white smock [petticoat], very clean and fair and it trailed in the dirt and her coat behind. And I took her coat and did carry it up a good way and then it hung too low before and I told her in talk she should do me a favour to let me wait on her. And she said I should. Then said I, I mean, madam, to wait upon you [i.e. have sex with you, with a pun on 'weigh'] and not under you that I may make this belly a little bigger [i.e. make you pregnant] to carry up this smock and coats out of the dirt. And so we talked merrily and then she began to lean upon me when we were past the dirt and to be very familiar with me. And methought she began to love me and when we were alone out of sight, methought she would have kissed me. And with that I waked. (Paster and Howard 1999, pp. 189–90.)

Document 2

A Midsummer Night's Dream contains more references to 'eyes' than any other Shakespeare play. Its action hinges on the balance between perception and reason and the fragility of our ability to distinguish apparent truth from falsehood, especially when passion or desire disrupts the eyes' ability to inform the reason. In *De Dignitate et Augmentis Scientiarum* (*Of the Worth and Growth of Knowledge*, Book 2, chapter 13), Sir Francis Bacon provided a vivid image of this battle:

> Tigers likewise are kept in the stables of the passions, and at times yoked to their chariot; for when passion ceases to go on foot and comes to ride in the chariot, as in celebration of its victory over reason, then is it cruel, savage and pitiless towards all that withstand or oppose it.

Folk customs and popular culture

Shakespeare includes in his play a number of motifs that recur in sixteenth century dream literature, such as the God of Love (a role absorbed by Oberon and Puck), an enchanted garden (the wood), journeying lovers and May morning. The precise timing of the action of Shakespeare's play is unclear (see Chapter 1): the young lovers and Bottom undergo their transforming experiences after Midsummer Night, but Theseus, coming across the four young people next morning observes 'No doubt they rose up early to observe / The rite of May'. (IV.i.131–2)

Document 3

Philip Stubbes, a pamphleteer with a strict moral bent, wrote an outraged, yet detailed, account of depravity in his *Anatomy of Abuses* (1583) which proved extremely popular, with a fourth edition appearing in 1595.

> Against May[day], Whitsunday, or other time, all the young men and maids, old men and wives, run gadding over night to the woods, groves, hills, and mountains, where they spend all the night in pleasant pastimes, and in the morning they return, bringing with them birch and branches of trees, to deck their assemblies withal, and no marvel, for there is a great lord present among them, as superintendant and lord over their pastimes and sports, namely Satan, Prince of Hell. But the chiefest jewel they bring from thence is their Maypole, which they bring home with great veneration. (Paster and Howard 1999, p. 109)

While stage and screen productions have placed different emphasis on the sexual activity of the young lovers, in Shakespeare's play, however intense the desires of the women are, they remain (apparently) chaste throughout their escapades in the wood, their relationships (along with Theseus' and Hippolyta's) being finally, and legitimately, consummated in the marriage bed. However, numerous popular ballads suggest a more active role for women as part of the Maying festivities, in which they sought a 'green gown', suggestive of sexual intercourse on the grass.

Document 4

From 'The Fetching Home of May, or, A Pretty new ditty wherein is made known, / How each lass doth strive to have a green gown', in *The Roxburghe Ballads*, vol. 3, part 1, edited and with notes by William Chappell (Hertford: Stephen Austin and Sons, 1875, pp. 312–17; reprinted in Paster and Howard, 1999, pp. 112–14; the following is an extract).

> The lads and the lasses,
> With scarves on their faces,
> So lively it passes,
> Trip over the downs:
> Much mirth and sport they make,
> Running at Barley-break:
> Good lack! What pains they take
> For their green gowns.

The ballad lists all the young men and women and the partners they each favoured, then goes on:

> Thus all the youngsters
> Had reached the green meadows
> Where they appointed to gather their May;
> Some in the sunshine, and some in the shadows,
> Singled in couples did fall to their play.

The final verses imagine gods and goddesses, many of whom figure in Shakespeare's play, indulging in the same sexual games. The ballad concludes:

> Cupid shoots arrows
> At Venus her darlings
> For they are nearest unto him by kind [inclination]:
> Diana he hits not, nor can he pierce worldlings,

For they have strong armour his darts to defend:
The one hath chastity,
And Cupid doth defy.
The other's cruelty
Makes him a clown.
But leaving this, I see,
From Cupid few are free,
And there's much courtesy
In a green gown.

Fairies

> When I was a boy our country people... were wont to please the fairies, that they might do them no shrewd turns, by sweeping clean the hearth and setting by it a dish whereon was set a [portion] of milk [soaked] with white bread, and did set their shoes by the fire, and many times on the morrow they would find a threepence in one of them. But if they did speak of it they never had any again.... That the fairies would steal away young children and put others in their places [was] verily believed by old women in those days, and by some yet living.
>
> John Aubrey (1688)

Fairies appear most frequently in English literature between 1570 and 1625, during which time many modern features of fairies were established. Shakespeare drew on a range of literary sources and popular folklore for his presentation of the spirit world, and, in turn, transformed some traditional attitudes (Lamb 2000 and Wall 2001 provide a good overview).

He took the name Oberon from an anonymous romance, *Huon of Bordeaux*, translated into English between 1533 and 1542. In this poem, Oberon's kingdom lies east of Jerusalem (an area known to medieval writers as India), where he and his fairies live in a wood, love hunting, and can create illusions of storms and other dangers or make mortals believe they are in Paradise. Oberon is described in the romance as being extraordinarily handsome and sexually attractive, and about three feet tall (though his stunted growth results from a curse). In Robert Greene's *James the Fourth* (c. 1590), where he also appears, he is 'not so big as the King of Clubs' on a playing card and 'tied to no place', with fairies like 'puppets that hopped and skipped'. But although many of the fairies in the play are clearly to be imagined as being very small, Oberon and Titania are both conceived of as similar in size to adult humans; indeed, are capable of sexual relations with them.

Before *A Midsummer Night's Dream*, Puck was a generic name for a small devil, a knavish sprite, a practical joker with a mocking sense of humour and the ability to change shape. Robin Goodfellow, on the other hand, was a folk figure rather than a fairy, whose traditional activities included leading humans astray, as if they were in a mist, changing shape and carrying out certain household tasks. All of these are absorbed into Puck/Robin in the play, but while Puck has often been made a female role, or played by a slightly built actor, traditionally Robin was broad-chested and taller than the average man: in Ben Jonson's masque, *Love Restored*, in which Robin is a leading character, he describes himself as an 'honest plain country spirit and harmless; ... he that sweeps the hearth and the house clean, riddles for the country maids, and does all their other drudgery while they are at hot cockles', and who is 'none of those subtle ones that can creep through at a key-hole or the cracked pane of a window. I must come in at a door'. Interestingly, in the light of his description of the mechanicals as 'hempen homespuns' (III.i.70) one of the tasks Robin performed was the onerous one of spinning the rough hemp fibres, and one of his catchphrases was 'What have we here? Hempton hampten, here will I never more tread nor stampen' (Lamb 2000, p. 295; also see Wall 2001 for a discussion of the significance of Robin/Puck's sweeping.) The woodcut illustration on the title-page of *Robin Good-Fellow, His Mad Pranks* (1628) in which, in addition to his broom and devil's horns, he sports a substantial erection, suggests he was, like Oberon, of human size, and it seems very likely too that he was originally played by an adult actor. The character of Robin appeared in numerous pamphlets, in one of which, *Tell-Truth's New-year's Gift* (1593) he wanted to help young women to marry men of their own choosing, not their father's. As many commentators have pointed out, Robin/Puck's actions also align him with the classical figure of Cupid: indeed, going 'to see the fairies' was a contemporary euphemism for seeking illicit sexual encounters.

Royal entertainments

Throughout her reign, Queen Elizabeth made 'progresses' (tours) through her kingdom, staying at great houses where she was often presented with pageants designed to celebrate her power and virtues as a ruler. In 1575 she visited Kenilworth, home of Robert Dudley, the earl of Leicester, whose star as the Queen's favourite (even, some thought, her lover) was soon to fade. The entertainment presented to her included a burlesque marriage provided by the 'lusty lads and bold bachelors' of the parish, and a spectacular water pageant featuring the figure of Arion, riding on a dolphin's back. If the 11-year-old Shakespeare was present, which as Kenilworth is within reach of Stratford is not implausible, he may later have recalled the sight when composing Puck and Oberon's shared recollection of a water pageant (II.i.148–54; and again, perhaps, when he wrote Twelfth Night, I.ii.11–16). Similarly, the moment when the amateur actor playing Arion sought to reassure the spectators that the sight was not magic by calling out that he was 'not Arion, but honest Harry Goldingham' might have swum back into Shakespeare's mind when he created Snug. There was also an amateur performance 'presented in an historical cue [style] by certain good-hearted men of Coventry' of the traditional Coventry Hock Tuesday play celebrating the battle to end Danish rule in the eleventh century. The performance was led by one Captain Cox, a mason by profession, who appears to have been admired by his fellows and also shared much of Bottom's confidence and powers of recall, including the story of Huon of Bordeaux (see above). Queen Elizabeth, however, proved a more generous patron to her players than Theseus.

Document 5

Robert Laneham, A Letter: Wherein part of the entertainment unto the Queen's Majesty at Killingworth Castle in Warwickshire in this Summer's Progress, 1575. [The description was printed, where and by who is not known, without an author's name attached.]

> But aware, keep back, make room now, here they come. And first, Captain Cox, an odd man, I promise you: by profession a mason and that right skilful, very cunning in fence, and hardy as Gawain, for his tonsord [broadsword] hangs at his table end. Great oversight [knowledge] hath he in matters of story, for as [example] *King Arthur's Book, Huon of Bordeaux* [...] *Colin Clout* [...] with many more than I rehearse here: I believe he have them all at his fingers' ends. ... Besides this [he is] of very great credit and trust in the town here, for he has been chosen alecunner

[ale taster] many a year [and] his judgement will be taken above the best, be his nose ne'er so red. [Laneham then describes the re-enactment of the battle and the victory.] This was the effect of this show, that as it was handled, made much matter of good pastime, brought all indeed into the great court, even under her Highness's window to be seen.

Elizabeth had, in fact, missed most of the performance as she was watching some dancing in her chamber. The queen:

commanded therefore on the Tuesday following to have it full out, as accordingly it was presented, whereat Her Majesty laughed well, [the actors] were the jocunder [merrier], and so much the more because Her Highness had given them two bucks [male deer] and five marks in money to make merry together; they prayed for Her Majesty, long, happily to reign, and oft to come thither that oft they might see her: and what, rejoicing upon their ample reward, and what, triumphing upon the good acceptance [reception], they vaunted [boasted] that their play was never so dignified [honoured], nor ever any players afore so beatified [blessed].

The entertainment offered to the Queen by Edward, Earl of Hertford, at Elvetham in 1591, not long before the play was written, offers further example of the frequency with which Elizabeth was figured as the Fairy Queen in literature and performance. Interestingly, the entertainment also included 'a more threatening image of the Fairy Queen, as Circe (also called "Titania" in Ovid's *Metamorphoses*), who reduced men to beasts with her wand', a tribute to her power that Elizabeth obviously welcomed, as she commanded that it be repeated three times (Paster and Howard 1999, p. 139).

Document 6

'*The Honourable Entertainment given to the Queen's Majesty in a Progress, at Elvetham in Hampshire, by the Right Honourable Earl of Hereford, 1591*', in Entertainments for Elizabeth I, *ed. Jean Wilson (Woodbridge: Brewer, 1980)*.

On the final day of her visit to Elvetham:

Her Majesty was no sooner ready and at her gallery window looking into the garden, but there began three cornets to play fantastic dances, at the measure [melody] whereof the Fairy Queen came into the garden

dancing with her maids about her. She brought with her a garland, made
in form of an imperial crown; within the sight of Her Majesty, she fixed
[the garland] upon a silvered staff, and sticking the staff into the ground,
spake as followeth:

I that abide in places underground,
Aureola, the Queen of Fairy Land,
That every night in rings of painted flowers
Turn round and carol our Eliza's name:
Hearing that Nereus [god of the sea] and the Sylvan [woodland]
gods [these are references to preceding pageants]
Have lately welcomed your Imperial Grace,
[I opened] the earth with this enchanting wand,
To do my duty to Your Majesty,
And humbly to salute you with this chaplet [a wreath of flowers, like
a crown],
Given me by Auberon, the Fairy King.
Bright shining Phoebe, that in human shape,
Hid'st heaven's perfection, vouchsafe t'accept it.

Again Elizabeth proved an appreciative audience member, dismiss-
ing the actors 'with thanks, and with a gracious largesse, which of
her exceeding goodness she bestowed upon them.'

In 1592, at Sudeley Castle in Gloucestershire, Daphne, seeking
protection from Apollo, flew to Elizabeth as the 'Queen of chastity',
and in Edmund Spenser's great poem *The Faerie Queen*, first published
in 1590, Elizabeth (Gloriana) was the Queen of Fairyland. Clearly a
direct parallel is not operating in Shakespeare's play (the humiliation exerted on Titania by Oberon would not have gone down well
if so), but it is interesting to note that in the 'dramatis personae' of
The Whore of Babylon (1607), Thomas Dekker's post-Gunpowder Plot
celebration of England's defeat of her catholic enemies, he drew an
explicit analogy: 'Titania, the Fairy Queen, under whom is figured
our late Queen Elizabeth'.

Theseus and Hippolyta

Document 7

Shakespeare took his framing story of Theseus and Hippolyta
from Chaucer's *The Knight's Tale*, which opens with the couple

waiting for their wedding and makes reference to the 'observance of May'.

> Stories of old have made it known to us
> That there was once a Duke called Theseus,
> Ruler of Athens, Lord and Governor,
> And in his time so great a conqueror
> There was none mightier beneath the sun.
> And many a rich country he hath won,
> What with his wisdom and his troops of horse.
> He had subdued the Amazons by force
> And all their realm, once known as Scythia,
> But then called Femeny. Hippolyta,
> Their queen, he took to wife, and, says the story,
> He brought her home in solemn pomp and glory.

Shakespeare found further elements of his plot and setting in the same tale, such as the rivalry of two young men, Palamon and Arcite, who fight in a grove for the love of Emilia, whom they first spy on a 'May-day morn' and whose duel in a glade in a wood is interrupted when Theseus, out hunting (which was 'his ruling joy and appetite'), accompanied by Hippolyta, comes upon them. (Chaucer, *The Canterbury Tales*, trans. Nevill Coghill, Penguin, 1951.)

Document 8

Plutarch's *Lives of the Noble Romans and Grecians* (translated by Sir Thomas North using the French version by Jaques Amyot). While Shakespeare drew the substance of his portrayal of Theseus as a great soldier from Chaucer, Plutarch offered a complex portrayal of the Greek ruler: on the one hand, a heroic, rational, statesman-like figure, the conqueror of the Minotaur and liberator of Crete; on the other, a serial womanizer, the ravisher of Helen, father of the ill-fated Hippolytus, and himself the unreliable son who, forgetting his promise to his father, Aegeus (who may have suggested Egeus to Shakespeare), to change his sails from black to white to signal his safe return, caused his grief-stricken father to leap to his death. The memory of his ill-fated son, Hippolytus exists in the play through the naming of Hippolyta (see Nuttall 2000).

Plutarch describes how, accompanied by his kinsman, Hercules, Theseus waged war against the Amazons:

> Afterwards, at the end of four months, peace was taken between them by means of one of the women called Hippolyta. For this historiographer calleth the Amazon which Theseus married Hippolyta, and not Antiopa. ... It is very true, that after the death of Antiopa, Theseus married Phaedra, having had before of Antiopa a son called Hippolytus.

Comparing Theseus with Romulus, Plutarch writes:

> Theseus' faults touching women and ravishments, of the twain, had less shadow and colour of honesty ... for he stole away Ariadne, Antiope, and Anaxo the Troezenian. Again, being stepped in years, and past marriage, he stole away Helen in her minority, being nothing near to consent to marry. Then his taking of the daughters of the Troezenians, of the Lacedaemonians and the Amazons ... did give men occasion to suspect that his womanishness [desire for women] was rather to satisfy lust than of any great love.

Amazons represented both the female warrior and the unruly woman, each of which turned the values of Elizabethan patriarchal society upside down. Paster and Howard (1999, p. 216) reproduce a Dutch engraving of 1598 of Queen Elizabeth I as a bare-breasted Amazon bearing a sword, and in which, when the image is turned on its side, the Queen becomes a map of Europe.

Transformation and translation

Publius Ovidius Naso (43 BC–17 AD) was a Roman poet whose work was extremely popular in Elizabethan England. His long poem, *Metamorphoses* (literally, 'changes of form'), is the most significant literary influence on the play, providing a framework for the various transformations caused by love, madness and imagination. Shakespeare drew extensively on George Golding's English translation, published in 1567, but while Ovid talks of Titania, Golding describes her only as 'Titan's daughter', which suggests that Shakespeare also used Ovid in the original as his source. Ovid refers to Titania five times: as Latona,

Circe, Pyrrah, Hecate and Diana in his telling of the story of Actaeon, whose fatal transformation into a deer when he observed Diana bathing is comically retold in Bottom's transformation to an ass. Reginald Scott, in his controversial *The Discovery of Witchcraft* (James I ordered the book to be burned) recounted the story of a young man turned into an ass who, like Bottom, wanted to eat only hay, but the most likely source was Lucius Apuleius' *The Golden Ass*, which captures the erotic dynamic found in Shakespeare's play.

Document 9

Lucius Apuleius, The Golden Ass, *translated by William Adlington, 1566 (subtitled* Metamorphoses, *and in which 'golden' means 'splendid').*

Lucius, hoping to turn into a bird, becomes an ass as a result of mistakenly using an ointment, his transformation being driven by his sexual desire as well as his curiosity:

> my hair did turn in ruggedness, and my tender skin waxed tough and hard, my fingers and toes losing the number of five, changed into hooves, and out of mine arse grew a great tail, now my face became monstrous, my nostrils wide, my lips hanging down, and mine ears rugged with hair: neither could I see any comfort of my transformation, for my members increased likewise, and so without all help (viewing every part of my poor body) I perceived that I was no bird, but a plain Ass.

Lucius rescues a young woman from danger, and she makes a fuss of him just as Titania and her fairies do Bottom:

> First I will bravely dress the hairs of thy forehead, and then I will finely comb thy main, I will tie up thy rugged tail trimly, I will deck thee round about with golden traps, in such sort that thou shalt glitter like the stars of the sky, I will bring thee daily in my apron the kernels of nuts, and will pamper thee up with delicates; I will set store by thee … thou shalt lack no manner of thing …

Lucius later finds himself in a sexual situation with a matron, and his description is not dissimilar to that of Bottom in Titania's bower, surrounded by four fairy helpers rather than four eunuchs:

> I am not able to recite unto you how all things were prepared: there were four eunuchs that lay on a bed of down on the ground with bolsters accordingly for us to lie on, the Coverlet was of cloth of Gold, and the pillows soft

and tender, where on the delicate matron had accustomed to lay her head. Then the eunuchs not minding to delay any longer the pleasure of their mistress closed the doors of the chamber and departed away: within the chamber were lamps that gave off a clear light all the place over: Then she put off all her Garments to her naked skin, and taking the lamp that stood next to her, began to anoint all her body with balm, and mine likewise, but especially my nose, which done she kissed me, not as they are accustomed to do at the brothel houses … for gain of money, but purely, sincerely, and with great affection, casting out these and like loving words: Thou art he whom I love, thou art he whom I only desire, without thee I cannot live, and other like preamble of talk as women can use well enough, when as they mind to show or declare their burning passions and great affection of love. Then she took me by the halter and cast me down upon the bed, which was nothing strange unto me, considering that she was so beautiful a matron, and I so well-boldened out with wine and perfumed with balm, whereby I was readily prepared for the purpose. But nothing grieved me so much as to think, how I should with my huge and great legs embrace so fair a matron, or how I should touch her fine, dainty, and silken skin with my hard hoofs, or how it was possible to kiss her soft, pretty and ruddy lips, with my monstrous mouth and stony teeth, or how she, who was young and tender, could be able to receive me.

And I verily thought if I should hurt the woman … I should be thrown to the wild beasts: But in the mean season she kissed me, and looked in my mouth with burning eyes, saying: I hold thee my cunny, I hold thee my nops, my sparrow, and therewith all she eftsoons [again] embraced my body round about, and had her pleasure with me. … She had a great abundance of hair dispersed and scattered about her neck; on the crown of her head she bare many garlands interlaced with flowers; in the middle of her forehead was a compass in fashion of a glass or resembling the light of the moon; in one of her hands she bare serpents, in the other, blades of corn, her vestment was of fine silk yielding divers colours, sometime yellow, sometime rosy, sometime flamey, and sometime dark and obscure, covered with a black robe in manner of a shield, and pleated in most subtle fashion … whereas here and there the stars glimpsed, and in the middle of them was placed the moon, which shone like a flame of fire, [and] round about the robe was a coronet or garland made with flowers and fruits.

Pyramus and Thisbe

Ovid's *Metamorhoses* provided Shakespeare with the inspiration for his play-within-a play as well as the tragic subjects for the plays Theseus rejects. Ovid's mulberry tree, under which the lovers agreed to meet, and whose 'fruit as white as snow' and leaves were stained 'a deep dark purple' with Pyramus' blood, becomes in the play love-in-idleness, the wild pansy, injured by Cupid's arrow.

Golding's translation is in 'fourteeners' (lines with fourteen syllables, rather than the ten of the iambic pentameter). This was the verse medium of much earlier Elizabethan drama, 'tragical comedies' such as *Appius and Virginia* or *Damian and Pithias* and bombastic tragedies like *Horestes* and Thomas Preston's *Cambises, King of Persia* (c. 1570). Shakespeare had earlier poked fun at Preston's play in *Henry IV Part 1*, when Falstaff entertains his cronies in the Boar's Head tavern by performing in 'King Cambises' vein' (II.iv). Indeed, Shakespeare probably also had in mind the sub-title of Preston's play (and many others like it) – *A Lamentable Tragedy, mixed full of pleasant mirth* – in the title of Quince's work.

Document 10

Ovid's lengthy poem draws on a wide range of classical myths, in particular those that are concerned with people transformed in some way, and which are often intensely erotic. In Ovid's story of Pyramus and Thisbe, the young lovers (not much more than children, in fact), whose 'houses joined so near / That under one roof well nigh both twain conveyed were', are prevented in their love by the opposition of their parents. With the flames of repressed love burning in their breasts, the lovers discover 'a cranny' in the wall that divides their houses:

> and made a way whereby
> To talk together secretly, and through the same did go
> Their loving whisperings, very light and safely, to and fro.
> Now, as at one side *Pyramus*, and *Thisbe* on the t'other,
> Stood often drawing one of them the pleasant breath from other,
> O, thou envious wall (they said), why letst [prevent] thou lovers thus?

They agree to meet at Ninus' tomb that night. Thisbe arrives first:

> But see the chance; there comes besmeared with blood
> About the chaps a lioness, all foaming, from the wood,
> From slaughter lately made of kine [animals], to staunch her bloody thirst
> With water of the foresaid spring, whom Thisbe spying first
> Afar by moonlight, thereupon with fearful steps gan fly …

And as she fled away for haste she let her mantle fall,
The which for fear she left behind, not looking back at all.
For when the cruel lioness her thirst had staunched well,
In going to the wood she found the slender weed [garment] that fell
From Thisbe, which with bloody teeth in pieces she did tear.

Pyramus arrives, and finding the scarf and thinking Thisbe dead:

he drew
His sword, the which among his guts he thrust, and by and by
Did draw it from the bleeding wound beginning for to die,
And cast himself upon his back.

Thisbe, returning, finds her lover, dead:

She beat her breast, she shriekèd out, she tore her golden hairs,
And taking him between her arms did wash his wounds with tears.
She meynt [mixed] her weeping with his blood, and kissing all his face
(Which now became as cold as ice) she cried in woeful case [tones]:
'Alas, what chance my Pyramus hath parted thee and me?
Make answer, O my Pyramus ...'
But when she knew her mantle there and saw his scabbard lie,
Without the sword, 'Unhappy man, thy love hath made thee die.
Thy love', she said, 'Hath made thee slay thyself. This hand of mine
Is strong enough to do the like ...'
That said, she took the sword yet warm with slaughter of her love
And setting it beneath her breast, did to her heart it shove.

4 Key Productions and Performances

The playhouses in London were closed by Order of Parliament in 1642, and professional playing all but ceased – certainly publicly – until the Restoration of Charles II in 1660. When the theatres reopened, a number of the defining characteristics of Elizabethan and Jacobean drama and theatre practice had changed or were coming under pressure to do so. Most striking to theatre-goers would undoubtedly have been the presence of actresses on the public stage, the absence of open-air playhouses, and the introduction of painted, changeable scenery on the stages of the intimate, indoor, candle-lit theatres that had survived the interregnum. The dearth of new plays, too, meant that those from pre-war days continued to provide the bulk of the repertoire, though often in radically altered adaptations and with someone else's name on the playbill, as the work of the earlier writers was so little known that the adapters were able to get away with their unacknowledged plagiarism.

Versions of *A Midsummer Night's Dream* not under the King's Men's control may even have been appearing before the closure. In 1624, John Gee, in *New Shreds of Old Shares*, refers to 'the comedy of Pyramus and Thisbe', and this, together with Charles I's reference to 'Pyramus and Thisbe' in his copy of the second Folio (1632) has led to speculation that it had become the practice to perform the mechanicals' play separately from the main play. Whatever the practice was before 1642, during the closure of the theatres the play was reduced to a 'droll' (a short, farcical performance) of 'Pyramus and Thisbe', presented at fairs and suchlike by travelling players. The genre of the droll survived the reopening of the playhouses, and the 30-page *The Merry Conceited Humours of Bottom the Weaver* was published in 1661 and again in the following year in *The Wits; Or, Sport upon Sport,* a 'Curious Collection of Several Drolls and Farces'. Interestingly, this droll states explicitly that not only is the doubling of Theseus/Oberon and Hippolyta/Titania possible, but that Bottom, Flute and Snout 'likewise may present three fairies', and it hints too that Pugg (Puck) may also play Egeus, an indication that these spirits were in this instance definitely to be played by adults.

On Michaelmas Day, Monday 29 September, 1662, Samuel Pepys attended a performance of *A Midsummer Night's Dream* at the King's Theatre, a visit which coincided with his decision to give up his self-imposed ban on drinking wine and going to plays. This might be expected to have put him in a good mood, but it proved not to be the case. As he wrote in his *Diary*, 'to the King's Theatre, where we saw *Midsummer Night's Dream*, which I had never seen before, nor ever shall again, for it is the most insipid, ridiculous play that I ever saw in my life'; indeed, 'all his pleasure' in the evening was derived from 'some good dancing and some handsome women.' We can't be certain what Pepys actually saw on stage, but a surviving version published to coincide with King Charles II's coronation, heavily adapted and comprising parts of the mechanicals' scenes and a reduction in the roles of the fairies, might give us some idea. In a sign of what was often to be their fate, the lovers were omitted altogether. Further evidence for what a late seventeenth century version of the play might have looked like is provided by two surviving texts marked up for performance. The first, intended for a theatre in Hatton Garden, covers only acts one to three: plot and mechanicals are privileged over poetry and other mortals, and Titania is omitted completely. Similar cuts are found in a text apparently destined for the playhouse in Smock Alley, and again demonstrate the preference for the mechanicals and general expendability of the lovers that one finds in later periods: 'the problematic areas of the seventeenth century remained problematic into the twentieth' (Griffiths 1996, p. 11). In 1692, a semi-operatic version of *A Midsummer Night's Dream* entitled *The Fairy Queen*, probably adapted by Elkanah Settle, with music by the celebrated composer Henry Purcell, and designed in part as a compliment to William III and Queen Mary, was staged at the Queen's Theatre (formerly the Dorset Garden Theatre). About half of Shakespeare's lines were cut (the remainder being modernised), as were as many characters and plot elements (including all references to Athens, Hippolyta and the wedding plans with which the play opens) and other parts transposed: the rehearsals and performance of *Pyramus and Thisbe* were placed in Act III for example.

A Midsummer Night's Dream was virtually absent from the stage for the first 50 years of the eighteenth century, and then only in the form of operatic adaptations, such as Richard Leveridge's *Comic Masque of Pyramus and Thisbe* (1716) – a satire on Italian opera while in an early example of inter-textuality, the mechanicals' play was included as an entertainment in *Love in a Forest*, itself an adaptation of *As You Like It*. Although the second half of the eighteenth century saw considerable interest in the works of Shakespeare and the publication of a number of major editions that sought to establish texts as close as possible to reliable earlier copies, such was not the attitude of those who put the plays on stage. David Garrick was the most celebrated actor of his day and a close friend of Dr Johnson, whose edition of Shakespeare was published in 1765. Garrick enjoyed a position of sufficient eminence in the theatre that had he wished to take a different course from the adapters of Shakespeare he could, but he chose not to do so: during his 30-year management of Drury Lane (1747–76) he produced three opera versions of *A Midsummer Night's Dream*, of which the most successful was the furthest from the original play, George Colman's 400 line version, *A Fairy Tale*.

The dominant mode of staging Shakespeare throughout most of the nineteenth century was pictorial. In 1840, the year Queen Victoria married Prince Albert, Lucia Elizabeth ('Madame') Vestris, who with her husband, Charles Mathews, ran the Covent Garden theatre, staged a production of *A Midsummer Night's Dream* in an adaptation by James Robinson Planché. Williams notes of the sensitive cutting of the text that it set the pattern for subsequent Victorian productions: 'shorten and soften the lovers' wrangles in the forest, remove arcane references, shorten lyrical elaborations that do not move the plot, omit any shade of the suggestive and any shadow of the unpleasant' (1997, p. 98). Madame Vestris played Oberon, the first woman to do so, wearing a costume designed to show to advantage her famously shapely legs (reproduced in Wells 2002, p. 261), so setting a tradition which lasted until 1914. The production employed a diorama to change the locations visually, including a slow sunrise over a lake, with the waning moon reflected in the water and fairies flying above the stage holding small lanterns. Mendelssohn's overture opened the production, and other songs were introduced, including setting 'I know a bank' to a melody, sung by Oberon and the First Fairy: this may perhaps have been one of the moments the young Queen Victoria was referring to when, having seen the production in February 1841, she wrote in her diary of 'those stupid duets and songs'. Three years later, Ludwig Tieck staged the play in Potsdam, with new incidental music by Mendelssohn – a production that stayed in repertoire in Berlin until it was eventually abandoned in 1885. Williams prints an illustration of the Potsdam production (1997, p. 106).

By the middle of the nineteenth century, productions in England were seeking increasing levels of historical detail in their staging, though they often did so without considering 'whether accuracy of period and locale were in any sense relevant to a visual understanding of the plays' (Kennedy 2001, p. 27). As Charles Kean found, however, when he staged *A Midsummer Night's Dream* at the Princess' Theatre, London, in October 1856, the play proved resistant to the archaeologically accurate approach he favoured – 'the general character of the play is so far from historical ... that I have held myself unfettered with regard to chronology' – and so he chose a later period in Athenian history. Audiences saw the panorama of ancient Athens, and an authentic workshop for Quince, complete with tools, Kean claimed, 'Copied from Discoveries at Herculaneum' (though many had already been used in an earlier production of *A Winter's Tale*). Kean cut around 40% of the text, replacing it with music, dance and the massive crowd scenes and tableaux, flying fairies, played against 'the exquisite scenery' (for which the water colour designs survive) that characterised his productions. Ellen Terry played Puck, and Kean cast a woman as Oberon but adults as the fairies. Illustrations of the production show Titania's fairies, wearing ballet dresses, their toes pointed, an influence from the romantic ballet, *Les Sylphides* (1832) that had employed a new technique of *pointe* dancing to suggest airy lightness.

*　*　*

Of the four productions discussed below, the first exemplifies the dominant mode at the close of the nineteenth century, while each of the following three represents a production that, by shifting the paradigm, has clearly influenced how *A Midsummer Night's Dream* – and Shakespeare generally – has since been performed.

Herbert Beerbohm Tree,
His Majesty's Theatre, London, 1900

Tree moved in to the new Her Majesty's theatre in Haymarket in 1897, having planned it himself, from the foyer to the private penthouse flat, and ran the theatre until 1913, gaining it a reputation for lavish productions of Shakespeare. In 1899 he appeared in the title role of King John in the first filmed extract of a Shakespeare play (see Chapter 5) and in 1904 he founded what became the Royal Academy of Dramatic Art. He was knighted in 1907 and died in 1917.

* * *

In 'The Living Shakespeare', a chapter in his book, *Thoughts and After-Thoughts* (1913), Tree addressed the question of the relationship between Shakespeare's plays and pictorial scenic design, arguing that audience response – measured by the box office; 220,000 people would see his production of *A Midsummer Night's Dream* – supported his belief in putting 'Shakespeare upon the stage as worthily and munificently as the manager can afford' (p. 43). The essay is clearly written in part to oppose the views of those who were advocating a return to 'Elizabethan' theatre practices (see below), which Tree dismissed as 'primitive' (p. 47) staging:

> We are assured that we are not to apply to Shakespearian productions the same care, the same reverence for accuracy, the same regard for stage illusion, for mounting, scenery, and costume, which we devote to authors of lesser degree; … in other words that we are to produce our national poet's works without the crowds and armies, without the pride, pomp, and circumstance which are suggested in every page of the dramatist's work, and the absence of which Shakespeare himself so frequently laments in his plays. (p. 43)

Tree started from the assumption that 'the entire business of the stage is – Illusion. … all that aids illusion is good, all that destroys illusion is bad' (p. 57), citing in evidence the play of *Pyramus and Thisbe* – 'the most tinglingly satirical skit on the primitive methods of the stage' (p. 65).

Tree's production opened on 10 January 1900, a significant date as Tree 'consciously intended that it should be a reaffirmation of traditions as the century clock turned twelve amidst the growing sense that an era was ending' (Williams 1997, p. 132). A souvenir programme contained a series of essays on aspects of the play and production, including one reflecting a much-advertised feature of Tree's production: the inclusion, for the first time of Mendelssohn's *complete* score in a stage production, which 'consists of twelve numbers: the Scherzo, Fairy March, a song ("You spotted snakes") for two sopranos and chorus, Melodrama, Intermezzo, second Melodrama, Notturne (sic), Andante, Wedding March, Allegro Commodo, Bergomask, Dance and Finale' (programme, p. 9; see Todd 2003).

The programme lists a total of 28 actors, but the costume list indicates a further 80 performers in the roles of fairies, attendants, guards, etc. Tree played Bottom, Helen Maud Holt, his wife (or Mrs Tree as she is named in the cast list), was Titania and, following the practice established by Madame Vestris, Oberon was played by a woman (Julia Neilson, a big star at the time). Puck, too, as in Kean's production, was a female part, and the Fairies were played by girls (except Peaseblossom who was played by Master Cyril Smith). The programme contains pictures of many of the actors in costume, and from these and surviving water colour designs (by Percy Anderson), it is possible to establish the way the production was dressed (though there is occasionally the not-uncommon discrepancy between the designer's drawings and the costumes worn by the actors). The mortals were all dressed in classical Greek style. Lysander, for example, is pictured as a young warrior, with studded breastplate, short tunic, laced soft-leather knee-length boots, short cloak pinned at the shoulder with a brooch, and wearing a sword. Demetrius is dressed in similar fashion, but with metal breastplate and cuirasses. Hermia and Helena each wore a long, loose dress with a shawl round the waist and draped over an arm. Hippolyta is shown in a full-length, layered robe, broad bracelets at her wrists and wearing an elaborate headdress, while Theseus has a formidable-looking helmet, breastplate and full cloak, and carries a staff of authority. The mechanicals are a pretty grotesque-looking group except for Bottom (Tree) who, pictured inside the programme's front cover, is dressed in a simple short tunic, with bare legs and sandals. Starveling appears to have affected a twisted body and limp to go with his bundle of sticks, lanthorn and (real) dog. Quince (pictured on the page with the cast list) holds a copy of his play and a quill pen and, with his bald domed head, hair long at each side and pointed beard seems to be an intentional echo of Martin Droeshout's engraving of Shakespeare that fronts the 1623 First Folio. Mrs Tree as Titania wears a simple dress and red feather head-dress, with wings, while Miss Neilson as Oberon wears an electrically illuminated spiked helmet and breastplate (with obvious echoes of Britannia), and a rather resigned expression. The costumes for the Fairies comprise tight-fitting tops and tights, with cloaks, wings and hats, though the sleek forms of the designs look slightly less so on the children photographed as a group. Interestingly, the critic of the *Pall Mall Gazette* offered a view on the contemporary popularity for a female Oberon, writing of Neilson's performance that 'Her Oberon is truly regal, while the mere fact of her being a woman just differentiates it from humanity' (quoted in Williams 1997, p. 137).

The play was divided into three acts and the prompt copy indicates that some 410 lines were cut, partly to make 'space' for changing the scenery that made descriptive language redundant. The curtain rose to reveal the exterior of Theseus' palace, designed by Joseph Harker, with 'Athens' inscribed in Greek in a cartouche suspended above and with Theseus and Hippolyta already discovered on stage. The detailed staging notes in the prompt copy indicate the opening action: 'Theseus kisses Hippolyta. Then, to music, entrance of four amazons crossing from L to right at back; Officer of the Guard Xes [crosses] to Theseus and hands scroll; court ladies and gentlemen; Egeus holding Hermia's arm.' For scene two, a change revealed Quince's workshop, with door and window at the rear and two benches, but a much longer change was required to set the following scene in the wood. It was here that Tree's production was particularly visually elaborate. With a setting by Hawes Craven (Tree used different designers for different acts of the play), a canopy of trees hung above the stage with, below, grass and even a stream of real water in which Bottom checked his reflection for the ass's ears on waking from his dream. It provided the iconic model – but also, with theatrical tastes changing, the whipping boy – of pictorial Shakespeare. Here, too, Tree employed a range of theatrical techniques: the prompt copy indicates the First Fairy enters from up-stage-left, 'from stream … on wire' (i.e., flying, as Puck also does later), and it notes too that 'dolls … fly', no doubt to give the impression of tiny air-born fairies (see Figure 24, Williams 1997, p. 135).

Music cues are extensive through the scene, as are those for birdsong and coloured light. The third act returns to Theseus' palace. To watch the mechanicals' play, Theseus and Hippolyta are placed on a raised dais, stage left and angled towards the audience, with Hermia and Lysander at the upstage end, Helena and Demetrius at the lower. The mechanicals, each apart from Bottom and Thisbe, carrying a placard, are positioned opposite them, stage right, on a similar angle, and the stage is filled with guards carrying lamps, amazons and ladies and gentlemen of the court.

Tree took full advantage of the most up-to-date stage lighting. At the end of their play, Theseus dismissed the mechanicals and the mortals exited to the strains of Mendelssohn's Wedding March. As the fairies entered, Oberon touched each of the pillars with his wand and they glowed from within, and, as 'the fairies steal away … slowly the light dies down … and, when all is darkness, the big curtain falls'. Critical responses were lavish with praise for the production's scenic effects, summed up by the *Athenaeum's* critic's view that 'no spectacle equally artistic has been seen on the English stage', with the production achieving 'what may, until science brings about new possibilities, be regarded as the limits of the conceivable'.

In April 1911, Tree (now Sir Herbert) staged the play again, although this time he employed only one set designer, and there were some cast changes, including a new Bottom – Arthur Bouchier – to replace Tree. The production was essentially the same, except, seeking even greater verisimilitude, Tree introduced his (in) famous live rabbits that followed trails of bran around the stage to the distraction of the audience and evident annoyance of cast and crew: at one point in the prompt copy the stage manager has written, in triply underlined capital letters in red ink that suggest his evident feeling, 'NO RABBITS'. No doubt Bouchier would have agreed – he carried a rabbit with him for the opening night curtain call, only for it to bite him.

*   *   *

In the 'After-Thought' to 'The Living Shakespeare', Tree acknowledged that fashions in theatrical styles inevitably change: 'Ragtime and Futurism are holding capital on our boards; but soon they too may be swept away into the limbo of the half-remembered' (1913, p. 72). In Germany, experiments had begun in non-illusionistic staging that sought to replicate Elizabethan practices, culminating in a 'Shakespeare Stage' in Munich in 1899. In England, William Poel had been campaigning since the early 1880s for a return to the comparatively simple theatre practice of Shakespeare's own time, his ambition being to perform Elizabethan drama 'under the conditions the play was written to fulfil' (see White 1998 in Further Reading).

Despite such innovations, audiences of *A Midsummer Night's Dream* at the turn of the century would have brought with them to the theatre a fixed set of expectations of what they would find: realistic, pictorial settings enhanced with any number of devices (of which live rabbits have become the metonym); extensive incidental music by Mendelssohn; children playing the fairies; an actress to play Oberon and generally Puck; and a heavily cut text (to make space for spectacle). In 1911, Tree still thought it artistically and economically profitable to stage such a production. Within a year, such a venture would seem an act of regressive folly.

Harley Granville Barker,
Savoy Theatre, London, 1914

William Poel's legacy resides less in his own considerable achievements than in the work and reputations of those he influenced and inspired. Among those was Harley Granville Barker who, in the early years of the twentieth century, though he directed only three Shakespeare plays (and was associated with a fourth in 1940) brought about a sea-change in approaches to Shakespearean staging.

Barker was born in London in 1877, and as a young actor appeared in productions mounted by Poel for his Elizabethan Stage Society. In 1912, however, while acknowledging Poel's achievements, Barker drew a crucial distinction between their approaches when, about to direct *Twelfth Night*, he wrote that, 'I don't go so far as Mr Poel; I think his method is somewhat archaeological; there is somewhat too much of the Elizabethan letter, as contrasted with the Elizabethan spirit.' *A Midsummer Night's Dream* was the third Shakespeare play Barker directed at the Savoy Theatre in London. The first, *The Winter's Tale*, opened on 21 September 1912, after which night, in Dennis Kennedy's words, 'Shakespearian production [would] never be the same' (1985, p. 123). Barker's approach could not offer a more radical alternative to that of his Victorian predecessors. *The Winter's Tale* was staged on a bright, white stage, extended by a forestage into the auditorium and illuminated by lights fixed to the dress circle. Instead of naturalistic images on painted backdrops, silk drops were decorated with non-realistic designs. *Twelfth Night* opened in November 1912. In comparison to the cool atmosphere of *The Winter's Tale*, this production was given a 'warmer' feel, though it was no less experimental in its look or its action, with designer Norman Wilkinson creating sets even less illusionistic than before. The production was a popular and (largely) critical success, and after a year working on other projects, Barker returned to Shakespeare with a production of *A Midsummer Night's Dream* that opened at the Savoy Theatre on 6 February 1914.

Barker hardly cut the text at all (no more than a handful of lines and occasional words) and added just one song at the end of the play; nor did he alter the sequence of the scenes. As Oberon he cast Dennis Neilson-Terry, the son of Julia Neilson who had played the part for Tree, and only the second male actor to play the role in 74 years, with another male actor, Donald Calthrop as Puck. The settings, again designed by Wilkinson, pursued the simple, clean lines of the earlier Savoy productions. The opening scene, Theseus' palace, set the Duke and Hippolyta on a decorated bench at the top of a rostrum approached by shallow steps and backed by a grey curtain with a larger-than-life grapevine pattern (not unlike a William Morris design). The costumes for the mortals were 'Greek' – plain or patterned robes with decorated hems for the 12 attendants, grouped either side of the stage, and more elaborate robes for the royal couple (also a tall crown for Theseus) and Philostrate, who carried a large staff of office. The change to scene two, here set in Quince's house, was effected by raising the grey curtain to reveal a pink one, painted with windows and doors, and the outline of the town's roofs. At the end of Act One, Barker introduced a five-minute break and (as he discusses in his *Preface* to the play) then ran through to Act Four without any interruption. The meeting of Oberon and Titania was played on the rostra used in the opening scene, but for the scene of her bower a curtain was raised to reveal a gentle mound (a clear echo of the formal dais of the opening scene) above which was suspended a wreath of foliage filled with fairy lights. From the centre of this hung a gauze cylinder, which could be used to conceal Titania while asleep without removing her from the stage (see p. 36). The backdrop was formed by a semi-circle of hangings, with provision for entrances, and painted in non-realistic woodland images, with strips of material for trees. The production employed no footlights. The scene was lit – not illusionistically – by 'frosted' light from the dress circle with coloured light added from the flies. The stage image overall gave the sense, in Christopher McCullough's apt phrase, 'of nature cased in the sensual lines of art nouveau patterns' (2008, p. 116).

At the end of Act Four, Barker inserted a 15-minute interval, after which the curtain rose to reveal Theseus' palace (only the third setting needed in Barker's production) but with a striking modernist formality. The rostrum from the opening was returned (or revealed), but a higher platform now ran across the back of the stage with seven substantial white columns decorated with simple black bands and, at their base, a repetition of the pattern that decorated the hems of the attendants' robes. A cyclorama at the rear of the stage provided a night sky, decorated with silver stars. At the point when Theseus decides which play he has chosen, four green and silver cushioned couches were placed in a gentle semicircle, following the curved line of the forestage. Theseus and Hippolyta reclined on a couch each, while the pairs of lovers shared the remaining two. The mechanicals performed on the raised platform at the rear of the stage (one photograph of the scene shows Pyramus and Thisbe kneeling either side of a brick-painted wall that sports a very noticeable hole), and while the arrangement removes the main focus of the scene – the inset play – to the rear of the stage, it does allow the onstage spectators to interrupt the action as in Shakespeare's text. The positions were reversed for the lively dance that concluded the play, with the mechanicals on the forestage and the court watching from the steps behind. The departure of the court was accompanied by torchlight before the fairies entered and danced, weaving around the pillars, dropping rose petals, until only one remained. The curtain fell, Puck spoke the epilogue in front of it, and exited to a final solitary trumpet note. One innovation went unnoticed by critics: in the closing scene, in addition to having Egeus present, Barker introduced Helena's father, Nedar (see p. 65), who though referred to in Act I, never appears in Shakespeare's text, as a silent counterpart to Egeus.

'Can even genius succeed in putting fairies on the stage?' Barker asked in his first, 1914, *Preface* to the play (written while he was in rehearsal), seeing the creation of the fairy world as 'the producer's test' (1993, p. 32). Barker was immediately clear on what he did *not* want to do: to try to *'realize* these small folk' and certainly not to use children He knew he wanted them to 'sound beautiful' (1993, p. 36) and be immediately recognised as different from the mortals. But how should they *look*? Barker wrote that the fairy king and queen seem to be 'romantic creations' with their origins in myth, or India, or some similar distant place, presumably taking as his starting point the references to Hippolyta and Oberon hailing from India, and to the changeling boy with whose mother Titania revelled 'in the spicèd Indian air by night'. His and Norman Wilkinson's solution was to make them entirely golden, fantastic creatures – Barker encouraged a friend to come to an early performance, before the gold leaf had a chance to rub off – who moved in a mechanistic manner, or stopped in frozen postures, unseen by the mortals. When the production was seen in New York, one critic dismissed the fairies as animated 'steam radiators', but for most observers the impression was definitely 'oriental' or Asian, with critics describing them variously as resembling 'ormolu fairies' or 'Cambodian idols', with Oberon looking like 'a quaint little golden idol from an Indian temple' or a 'painted graven image'. Colour photographs (reproduced in Williams 1997) that survive of Oberon and Titania with their fairy attendants give a good idea of their startling appearance, both with high fantastic crowns, a silver train for her, gold for him, highly decorated shoes, and he with bare legs bound round with what look like precious stones. A monochrome production photograph of the encounter between Oberon and Titania, and one of an individual fairy show the futuristic, almost science fiction feel that the costuming achieved (reproduced in Williams 1997, p. 149). On the other hand, and clearly to stress the 'strangeness' of these fairies, Barker wanted Puck to echo English folklore (1993, p. 36), and he was dressed in vivid scarlet, wore a short wig of yellow hair, with the actor stressing the mischievous, joke-playing aspects of the character.

Barker dropped Mendelssohn's incidental music that had become embedded in the play as if it really were part of Shakespeare's invention (two trumpet fanfares, two minutes apart, replaced Mendelssohn's overture), and turned to the folk music specialist Cecil Sharp for the music and the choreography – both of which Barker insisted 'should have no truck with a strange technique brought from Italy in the eighteenth century' (1993, p. 36) but be

English. Sharp chose folk music, which, Barker thought suitable for *A Midsummer Night's Dream* (but not for Shakespeare generally), since it 'must have sounded familiarly in Shakespeare's ears, as it still, at first hearing, sounds somehow familiar to us' (1993, p. 53; he discusses his thoughts on music in general, and Sharp's solutions, in more detail in this extended *Preface* he wrote on the play in 1924, ten years after his production).

If *Twelfth Night* had restored some of the faith of those who had criticised *The Winter's Tale*, initial reviews of the production of *A Midsummer Night's Dream* were mixed, with critics divided about those aspects they enjoyed or disliked. Inevitably, with a production that departed so radically and thoroughly from the recent traditions of staging Shakespeare, even after the two preceding Savoy productions, some found it difficult to absorb all aspects of the production, with the innovations in staging, costuming, lighting, settings, in Barker's own words, 'stepping too boldly between Shakespeare's spirit and yours' and obscuring the play itself.

Barker had not eliminated the pictorial from future productions of this play (see Griffiths, Halio, Williams) but he had ensured that a new, modernist aesthetic would continue to challenge them. A paradigm shift had occurred.

Peter Brook, Royal Shakespeare Company, Stratford-upon-Avon, 1970

When Barker's production of *A Midsummer Night's Dream* went to America in 1915, he explained his visual approach: 'What is really needed is a great white box'. Half a century later, a production with a white set, a live rabbit and no Mendelssohn incidental music might suggest either homage to Tree and Barker or a post-modern ironic take on past productions. In fact, these were all elements of Peter Brook's legendary production (except for the rabbit, which was sacked early on). Drawing on or rejecting (however consciously) the play's production history, Brook was clearly influenced by continental European theatre practitioners such as Meyerhold, Piscator and Brecht and by the Polish director, Grotowski, and the Polish critic, Jan Kott (see pp. 139–41) – whose writings on the play had already influenced other directors (see Williams 1997, pp. 215–22).

The result, for many who saw Brook's production, was that he had not only rethought this particular play in its entirety but had also, in the words of one critic, created a 'historic landscape in the interpretation of Shakespeare's plays' in general (Robert Speaight, *Tablet*, 12 September 1970).

As usual, how to represent the spirit world presented a major problem. In his detailed diary of the preparation period and rehearsal process, David Selbourne notes that Brook would not let the term 'fairies' be used in rehearsal, preferring the (less fey?) word 'spirits', but the issue of the magic created by those spirits was central to his conception. In an interview in the *Daily Telegraph* (14 September 1970), Brook explained his approach:

> [T]oday we have no symbols that can conjure up fairyland and magic for a modern audience. On the other hand there are a number of actions that a performer can execute that are quite breathtaking. So we went to the art of the circus and the acrobat because they both made purely theatrical statements. We've worked through a language of acrobatics to find a new approach to magic that we know cannot be reached by 19th century conventions.

The programme for the production included a quotation taken from Brook's own book, *The Empty Space*: 'Once the theatre could begin as magic: magic at the sacred festival, or magic as the footlights came up. Today it is the other way round. … We must open our empty hands and show that really there is nothing up our sleeves. Only then can we begin' (1968, pp. 108–9). To house this physical magic, designer Sally Jacobs created a three-sided white box (as Granville Barker had suggested), producing a setting that has become one of the iconic images of late twentieth century Shakespearian production. Frequently likened to a squash court, but with clear echoes of an Elizabethan stage, the set had walls about 18 feet high with a gallery running round the top, accessed by ladders at the downstage edge of each wall, from which actors could observe the action below and, where necessary, help with the staging, throwing down blue foil 'lightning bolts', for example, at the first encounter between Oberon and Titania. At stage level, two narrow doors in the rear wall provided access. Trapezes were hung from the flies on which Oberon and Titania (doubled with Theseus and Hippolyta), Puck (doubled with Philostrate) and the four fairies (played by adult actors) could hover. Titania's bower was a bed of vermilion-coloured ostrich feathers lowered to the stage and raised up again, and the wood was created by large coils of wire in which characters could easily be snared. There was no attempt to hide the mechanism to achieve the effects. Music – or rather sound – by composer Richard Peaselee, was created using a mix of instruments (mainly percussive), found objects and, at times, long tubes of plastic (known as Free-Kas) that made noises when swung through the air.

The vivid colours of the costumes stood out against the white walls, also accentuating the physical forms of the actors. Lysander and Demetrius each wore a simple smock and loose trousers, Hermia and Helena simple, long dresses, all in a similar tie-dye fabric. Oberon and Titania wore silk robes – his purple, hers green – with Puck in a yellow silk 'clown suit' and blue skull-cap. The mechanicals were dressed in 'modern-day', working men's clothes – trousers, boots, with their braces over their vests. The fairies wore simple grey costumes that allowed them to be less visible than the brightly coloured characters.

Kott's influence was seen especially in the treatment of the relationship between Titania and Bottom as the ass: with Mendelssohn's Wedding March blasting out, Bottom was carried shoulder high to Titania's bower by her fairies, one of whom thrust his arm between Bottom's legs to simulate a huge erection, leaving little doubt as to what would transpire in the privacy of the bower: Brook explained that 'It is as though … a husband has secured the largest truck driver for his wife to sleep with to smash her illusions about sex and to alleviate the difficulties in their marriage' (quoted in Williams 1997, p. 227; also see p. 60 above).

For Brook (and for Supple, later; see below), 'The nineteenth-century tradition assumes that because people are workmen they are comic and empty-headed and they're to be laughed at, [but] … there's nothing in the text that suggests they are stage-yokels from the country' (quoted Williams 1997, p. 231). Consequently, the mechanicals, and their play, were taken seriously (too seriously for some, who considered Brook's *Pyramus and Thisbe* the least funny they had seen).

At the close, as Puck said his final lines – 'Give me your hands, if we be friends, / And Robin shall restore amends' (V.i.427–8), the actors left the stage and entered the auditorium to shake hands with the audience, emphasising Brook's notion of theatre as a shared experience.

Although positive responses were by far in the majority, praise for the production was not unanimous. In *Free Shakespeare*, John Russell Brown dismissed it as a bag of directorial tricks that ignored the text, Peter Fiddick (*Guardian*), wrote that 'at times ... you suspect that Shakespeare is being milked for some spice, or – as in the final incantation – solemnity, which signifies nothing', while Orson Welles noted that he was 'one of the two or three people in the world who don't like that production. As a production it's remarkable, but it's an insult to the play' (Mark W. Estrin, *Orson Welles: Interviews*, 2002, p. 147). David Selbourne's diary describes a rehearsal process at times less open to the creative energies of the actors and more constrained by the director's vision. On the other hand, despite its physical energy and inventiveness, Irving Wardle wrote in the *Times* that 'I have never heard it spoken with more scrupulous attention to sense and music', and that matches my own response to the production as a vibrant combination of gesture, physical action, voice and sound that opened up the play (despite my questions of Brook's [over]-reliance on Kott) and Shakespearian production in new and thrilling ways.

For many audiences and directors, Brook had shifted the paradigm once more: the burden of reinterpretation now fell on all subsequent directors, as critics began to categorize productions as 'Brookian' or 'non-Brookian' and, especially in the USA, many directors followed Kott's vision of a dark and menacing sexual world, though often at the cost of humour.

*　*　*

In his valuable study of changing approaches to staging Shakespeare in the twentieth century, Dennis Kennedy identifies the response to the colonial and post-colonial experience as a – perhaps *the* – defining focus of Shakespeare at the millennium. He discusses as an example the German director Karin Beier's 1995 production in Düsseldorf, described by her as 'European Shakespeare', that brought together 14 actors from nine countries who, with no shared common language, rehearsed and performed in their own language, to create in Kennedy's words 'a Babel of miscommunications from Europeans trying to be one' (2001, p. 329). In 2006, a production of *A Midsummer Night's Dream* approached the play with a similar level of linguistic complexity.

Tim Supple, the Swan Theatre,
Stratford-upon-Avon, 2006

Although reviewers of productions of *A Midsummer Night's Dream* have often evoked comparison with Brook's, none has been made more confidently than with Tim Supple's production, staged at the Swan in Stratford-upon-Avon in 2006 as part of the RSC *Complete Works* season, in which all Shakespeare's plays were staged in productions by the company itself and others drawn from around the world. At the invitation of the British Council, Supple – who sees *A Midsummer Night's Dream* as Shakespeare's 'most perfectly composed play' – spent months criss-crossing India and Sri Lanka auditioning and assembling a company of actors, musicians, designers and technicians. After a seven-week rehearsal period in Kerala, Southern India, the production opened in New Delhi, going on to Mumbai, Chennai and Kolkata before arriving in England.

Earlier productions of the play (such as Barker's and Brook's) had borrowed from Asian theatre forms and associations, but Supple's was the first to be set in India and performed by Asian actors. Indeed, Supple saw the production as expressing certain realities of life in modern India – 'multilingualism, the range of traditional practice and also what you might call metropolitan practice'. To all involved, working in so many languages was both challenging and liberating. No lines of the original were changed, and the text was translated faithfully into six languages other than English (Hindi, Bengali, Malayalam, Sinhalese, Tamil and Marathi). Two characters (Helena and Hermia) spoke English throughout, some (e.g., Theseus/ Oberon, Demetrius, Bottom) spoke their first language and English, and a few actors (such as Egeus and some in minor roles) spoke no lines in English. The shifts from one language to another underlined how easily in the play characters at odds with each other fail to connect, with (for those in the audience who understood the English only) the Shakespearean lines achieving a greater potency by their contrast with the other languages being spoken. There were other benefits too: as Chandan Roy Sanyal (Lysander) observed, the Indian languages influenced how the actors spoke Shakespeare in English: 'I enjoyed doing some of Shakespeare with the lyrical sweetness of Bengali'. To many in a predominantly English-speaking audience, aided by the careful interjection of enough lines in English to help spectators keep their bearings and an extensive plot synopsis in the programme, the play is sufficiently well known to present few problems in following it. The production was visually stunning, but as Michael Billington observed, 'although a ravishing spectacle, this is a production rooted in textual understanding' (*Guardian*, 9 June 2006).

With language fulfilling a different role, greater emphasis was necessarily placed on the skill and clarity of the actors' physical performances. Supple's previous work had demonstrated his interest and skill in theatrical storytelling: writing of his 1998 production of *Haroun and the Sea of Stories* one critic had identified the hallmarks of his work overall as 'spellbinding group tableaux, musical harmonies … explosions of colour and light and fabric … gesture and song'. The range of Indian theatre and dance forms employed was as diverse as the cast, drawing on bharatanatyam (the oldest of all Indian classical dance forms), kalarippayattu (a traditional martial art from Kerala), malkhamb (an ancient acrobatic art, often performed on poles or ropes), therukoothu (street theatre from the state of Tamil Nadu), bhangra (folk dance and music from the Punjab) and kathakali (the classical dance drama of Kerala). Brook too had sought inspiration from other cultures' performance practices but whereas they were then learned by his European cast, here they were the natural skills of Supple's performers.

The design by Sumant Jayakrishnan (set) and Zuleikha Chaudhari (lighting) presented the audience (there is no curtain at the Swan) with the thrust stage entirely covered with blue-grey silk. At the rear of the stage a wall of paper rose from the stage to the theatre roof, with a small jutting platform about two thirds of the way up, level with the first gallery of audience. Downstage centre stood a small trough of water and a Sivalinga stone, an emblem of Siva (with, to some, phallic connotations) which, when rubbed by Puck with wet fingers, created a haunting musical note that marked the beginning of the performance and the release of its magic. At the end of the first scene, the silk was abruptly pulled away through a small door to reveal the stage floor covered to a depth of several inches in reddy-brown earth for the mechanicals' scene, and which remained for the rest of the performance. As the mechanicals exited, the figures of the fairy world burst through the paper, to reveal a bamboo frame on which characters could hang or sit to observe the action. It was an image that for many Indian critics evoked a crowded modern city tenement, but one that also emphasised that the membrane that separates spirit and mortal worlds is fragile and easily breached, that the two are interlinked, an image also driven by Supple's view of the play as 'a series of trapdoors in which the characters are propelled into another existence'.

In the forest, the fairies controlled the staging and created each setting. The 'roundel and a fairy song' that Titania calls for became an aerial ballet, and as Oberon cast his spell while anointing Titania's eyes red cloths were lowered from the flies in one of which the sleeping queen was wrapped, as if in a cocoon, before being gently pulled up above the stage. The fairies created the 'green plot' and 'hawthorn brake' for the mechanicals' rehearsal (III.i), and when Bottom's companions fled, and he sang to keep up his spirits, Titania was gently lowered to the stage, the red cloth now making a hammock in which they could both lie. The 'drooping fog as black as Acheron' in III ii was represented by strips of elasticated rubber, stretched by Puck between posts that he set at the edges of the stage, to make a web in which the lovers became increasingly entwined, and when, worn out, they slept, each was wrapped, as Titania had been, in red cloth and raised above the stage. It was as if a state of sleep, or dream, was represented by floating above the ground. For the final scene, Puck marked areas on the earth floor with white powder before laying silk and flower petals on the earth, to create the positions from which the courtiers watched the play. Finally, in the closing moments Theseus and Hippolyta once again were transformed to Oberon and Titania, the Sivalinga stone was covered, the company filled the stage, singing and bearing torches, and the play ended.

I hope this brief summary of the staging might convey something of those qualities that led critics generally to praise the production's ravishing visual impact which, with its close attention to textual nuances, produced its vibrant mesh of words and images. At the same time, much of its strength derived from a beauty in simplicity, its (and the playwright's) trust in an audience's ability to engage its imagination with that of the performers. A case in point is how the transformation of Theseus and Hippolyta into Oberon and Titania was handled through the use of music and dance and how, in the final scene, the royal spirits first simply shed one costume for another (coat hangers lowered from the flies to help the change) before being handed bows (simple pieces of curved wood) to become their mortal counterparts in the hunt.

Supple has argued that 'a Shakespeare production should seek to reflect the time and place in which it is made with vivid honesty', and many aspects of the play were strengthened and given immediacy by the play's Indian context. The three interlinked worlds were precisely caught. The lovers (in critic Charles Spencer's words) were 'gorgeous in their silks, like the stars of Bollywood movies', before, in the case of the young quartet, they gradually shed their clothes in the forest and the young men in particular became entirely subject to their rampant sexual desire. The mechanicals were precisely individualised, like the tradesmen one sees in any Indian city or village, and the fairies resembled 'faintly menacing street performers' – indeed, the nine year-old boy who played the Indian boy, the changeling, was a street acrobat. Other elements of the play, too, seemed more potent in this setting, such as the arranged marriage contested by Hermia, and, crucial for this play, the constant co-presence of the mundane and spiritual. The production stressed not only the erotic dimension of the play, but its raw and at times violent sexuality. Supple was not, of course, the first to do this: Brook had rendered the encounter between Bottom and Titania as uncompromisingly sexual (see above) and Michael Boyd's 1999 production saw the play as a savage fertility rite and put on stage ideas also raised in a number of sexually oriented critical studies (see Chapter 6). Supple, however, while sustaining its comedic structure, also released the play's dark and often threatening sexual energy.

As Brook had done, Supple took the mechanicals seriously. These men may not be actors, but they *are* craftsmen, so the production treated as seriously as they did, their efforts to stage their play. The presentation took advantage, too, of the sharper class and caste distinctions in Indian society to reveal new insights: the workmen's concern not to frighten or offend the ladies of the court appeared misjudged when applied to the warrior queen, Hippolyta, or the sexually free antics of the young courtiers. More specifically, and in particular through the character of Flute, Supple offered an image of the transforming magic of the theatre: from a young man uncertain of his masculinity and saying his lines without sense, to one already dressed in his costume before the others and with the confidence to correct Quince's malapropism, to an actor unafraid of his own femininity, turning Thisbe's lines into a heartfelt, and moving, expression of grief. It was, for the character, an experience akin to ours as an audience who, as Supple believes, are transformed through the magical effect of performance.

5   The Play on Screen

A Midsummer Night's Dream has been adapted for cinema and television more than 30 times, and so this chapter will of necessity have to be very selective. (See Douglas Lanier, 2007, for an extensive discussion of the wide range of adaptation of the play in different print and electronic media.) I shall concentrate on filmed or televised versions of *A Midsummer Night's Dream* itself, but the play has also frequently been appropriated by a range of films for very different purposes, such as Woody Allen's *A Midsummer Night's Sex Comedy* (1982), Peter Weir's *Dead Poets Society* (1989), Tommy O'Haver's teen-flick, *Get Over It* (2001), and Gil Cates Jr's *A Midsummer Night's Rave* (2002), which in turn draws its cast from a range of teen movies in a plot loosely woven from Shakespeare's play. Though brief, perhaps the most intriguing example of this kind of appropriation is Powell and Pressburger's *A Matter of Life and Death* (1946), in which a dead pilot, played by David Niven, finds himself in heaven, where he witnesses a rehearsal of *A Midsummer Night's Dream* involving a cast of British and American airmen that offers a rare insight into different contemporary, and national, attitudes to how Shakespeare should be performed. The play has also attracted makers of animation films, notably the Czech director Jir' Trnka's brilliant 1959 version and, more recently, the version included in the first series (1992) of the excellent Welsh-Russian co-produced *Animated Tales from Shakespeare*.

The silent era

Early film-makers, conscious of a real or perceived notion that the new medium was seen by many as rather down-market, turned to Shakespeare to provide a sense of respectability. In 1909 *A Midsummer Night's Dream* became one of the first Shakespeare plays to be filmed (Beerbohm Tree's stage production of *King John*, ten years earlier, of which only one short fragment survives, being the first) when Charles Kent and J. Stuart Blackton directed a one-reel version for the American Vitagraph Company. Their film is not dependent on a stage source but offered 'as a separate art form whose neglect of the spoken word was amply compensated by an impressive range of other representative and performative strengths' (Buchanan 2005, p. 124). Though clearly shot largely during the summer in locations around New York City ('chosen with a special view to their harmony with the theme' in the words of an early review), the film was not released until Christmas Day 1909, a date presumably chosen to match the original play's festival connotations, if in a different season. It proved to be one of Vitagraph's most successful films.

Required to condense the plot, the directors compressed the play into 'a continuous and intelligible story which does not destroy the narrative' (quoted by Rothwell 2004, p. 11). The surviving print lasts just 11 minutes, though it seems that the opening titles and an early scene with Egeus, Theseus and the lovers may have been lost, as the surviving film opens with II.ii in the play. Although a caption following the sequence where Bottom describes his 'dream', announces that 'The Duke, Hippolyta and the lovers are married. The tradesmen give their play in honor of the occasion', the marriage is not in fact shown. The last scenes at court are evidently shot in a studio, and played against a painted backdrop. Costumes are Greek in style (and not dissimilar to those designed for Tree's production; see Chapter 4).

Inevitably some of the actors cope better than others with the demands of performing a text play with no sound, but all are helped by sub-titles that describe the up-coming action. As well as the use of locations, the film takes advantage of its unique ability to create moments of 'magic': simple stop-motion sequences allow Puck (Gladys Hulette) to appear and disappear, and, when ordered to circumnavigate the earth in search of the magic flower, Puck is first hoisted into the air, the image cuts to a shot of her 'flying' above a revolving roller painted as a map of the world, before she swoops (rather bumpily) down again to earth. The mechanicals' scenes are given prominence, with William V. Ranous, as Bottom, delivering a particularly energetic performance. As we have seen, it was common in nineteenth century stage productions, where fairyland had been predominantly the domain of women and children, to cast a woman in the role of Oberon (and Tree would continue the tradition two years after the film's release, in the revival of his 1900 production). But in the Vitagraph film, and without any explanation, a new female character, Penelope, is created, though she has no discernible connection to the Greek wife of Odysseus, famed – unlike Oberon – for her patience and fidelity. Whereas in the nineteenth century theatre this casting owed something to Victoria's presence on the throne, it is not apparent to me why this substitution should have been made in this case. Judith Buchanan ponders whether, given that the film retains the play's 'forgeries of jealousy' and sexual humiliation of Titania, 'a same-sex love might not be being delicately suggested' (2005, p. 125). But early film-makers, mindful of their wish to make their work culturally respectable, were alert to possible censorship – a year earlier, for example, the censors had been outraged by the shortness of the tunics worn by the actors in the Vitagraph film of *Julius Caesar* – and Rothwell's suggestion that the substitution of Penelope for Oberon might have been made because 'the director feared that the pedophile (sic) subtext about the Indian boy might upset the censorious classes' (2004, p. 10) may be nearer the mark.

* * *

Two further silent versions of *A Midsummer Night's Dream* were made in 1913. In Germany, the Danish director, Stellan Rye, made *Ein Sommersnachtstraum*, with a screenplay by himself and Hanns Heinz Ewers (who specialised in fantasy, mysticism and eroticism) that updated the story to the present day, and was shot in a 'sumptuously grandiose style' (Brode 2000, p. 62). The other film was directed in Italy by Paulo Azzuri, and has been seen as a possible influence on the first sound film of *A Midsummer Night's Dream*, made in 1935.

Shakespeare and Hollywood
1: Reinhardt and Dieterle (1935)

By the time the Austrian director, Max Reinhardt, made his film of *A Midsummer Night's Dream*, he was perhaps the most celebrated theatre director in Europe and America, and had produced Shakespeare's comedy in about 15 different versions between 1905 and 1934, often re-working it to suit his shifting sense of staging. His first production (in Germany in 1905), employed a revolving, three-dimensional forest and (as he did in all his productions) Mendelssohn's music, and was so successful that it earned him the directorship of the Deutsches Theater in Berlin. Productions followed in Austria, Italy, England, and in America to where he emigrated in 1933, following the rise of the Nazi party in Germany. A spectacular open-air production staged at the Hollywood Bowl in September 1935 (following outdoor productions in Florence 1933, and Oxford 1934), was partially underwritten by the film studio, attracted audiences in their thousands, and brought Reinhardt and his production – and their commercial potential – to the attention of Jack Warner, boss of the Warner Brothers Studios.

Reinhardt had made two silent films in 1913 (both of which took reality and imagination as their theme and one of which involved a dream scene), but the studio appointed Reinhardt's former pupil, William Dieterle, a more experienced filmmaker, as his co-director. Warner also gave the film encouraging production support: a budget of $1,500,000, a vast sound stage, and a cast including many household names, such as James Cagney (Bottom), Joe E. Brown (Flute), Victor Jory (Oberon) and Dick Powell (best known for his work in musicals) as Lysander, as well as rising stars Olivia de Havilland as Hermia (her first major screen role) and the 14-year-old Mickey Rooney as Puck, both of whom had appeared in Reinhardt's Hollywood Bowl production. They also drafted in all the available dwarves in Los Angeles to make up the orchestra of elves and goblins that had featured since Reinhardt's first production 30 years earlier.

The spectacular procession that opened the film would not have looked out of place in a stage production by Charles Kean or Beerbohm Tree, or, indeed, in a Cecil B. de Mille film epic. As Mendelssohn's overture swells in the background, a poster announces Theseus' forthcoming wedding and a competition for a prize for the best actors in a play celebrating the event. Lines of trumpeters play as Theseus disembarks from his ship and processes through Athens, while, taking advantage of film's ability to control the spectator's gaze in a way not easy on a crowded stage, the camera picks out key players in the crowd, signalling their relationships – the triumphant Theseus with the defeated Hippolyta, a large snake coiled round her body; Hermia and Lysander waving to each other (he, in armour, perhaps suggesting he too has returned from the war?); Hermia looking angrily at Demetrius, Helena gazing at him longingly; Quince and his fellows already busily planning what they will offer as entertainment.

The film is at its most spectacular in its treatment of the fairy world, including extensive use of music (much of it played on screen by that orchestra of gnomes and elves), song, and dance choreographed by Bronislawa Nijinskaya, Nijinsky's sister. Indeed, a good proportion of the film's 132 minutes running time is taken up with production numbers – ballet-like sequences involving Titania and her fairies – that have strong echoes of earlier stage productions (compare, for example, the illustration of Charles Kean's fairies in Griffiths 1996, p. 30, with a still from the film in Buchanan 2005, p. 130, and the similarities are immediately apparent). Our first view of the forest (created with 67 truckloads of greenery), to a background of Mendelssohn's score, shows Puck emerging from a heap of leaves while Titania's fairies, ethereal figures with gauze wings, dance around a tree in the mist before gradually spiralling up into the air to disappear while, as Puck and the First Fairy tell us of Oberon and Titania's quarrel over the Indian boy, the child himself appears, dressed in silks and a turban. Laurence Olivier once observed that while Shakespeare can reasonably ask the spectators to use their imaginations and 'piece out' a production's limitations with 'their thoughts' (*Henry V*, Prologue), a film by its very nature can – and should – actually show things. So, here, for example, when Puck chases the terrified mechanicals from the wood he actually takes on the form of a hound, a hog and a fire.

But as a number of critics have observed, as well as looking back, the film also prefigures later interpretations by exposing a darker, more ominous strand in the play, often drawing on conventions of horror films such as *Dracula* (1931). Bottom shakes with terror when he realises he has an ass's head, and Victor Jory, already established as a screen 'heavy', mainly in Westerns, here dressed in black with a crown made of gnarled tree branches, and accompanied by bats for attendants and mounted on a black horse, emphasised Oberon's capacity for malevolence, delivering his opening lines to Titania as a sinister threat. A sense of the film's style can be gained from the sequence (developed from a moment in Reinhardt's staging of the play in Oxford in 1934) where Oberon arrives to wake Titania. The gnome orchestra plays Mendelssohn's Nocturne while the First Fairy, in a shimmering costume and rabbit ears, dances a *pas de deux* with one of Oberon's bat-like servants, a duel between Moonlight and the Night that represents the erotic struggle between Oberon and Titania. Moonlight is powerless to escape, and Night bears her up into the sky, symbolising his victory over her and the reconciliation of the fairy king and queen. At that moment, Oberon himself, wearing a crown of silver and antler-like twigs, appears in the sky in a black chariot with swirling streamers of black cloth, his shadow covering his queen, the sleeping Bottom and the four lovers, while Titania and Oberon's followers dissolve into his cloak.

The performance of *Pyramus and Thisbe*, like the earlier scenes with the mechanicals, contains some good jokes but suffers – as it often does on stage – from the actors trying too hard to make it, rather than allowing it to be, funny, and as a result the humour is lost, and the court audience slip away before the bergomask, to the dismay of the amateur company who return to find the hall empty. Oberon and Titania appear behind gauze, with their fairies, to bless the house and marriages, before Puck blows out the lights and delivers his epilogue through an opening in the gauze that then closes, and the film ends.

The film was generally a success with American critics, and it marked a clear step forward from the first Shakespeare sound film, the 1929 version of *The Taming of the Shrew* starring Douglas Fairbanks and Mary Pickford. That had essentially been a filmed stage performance, whereas Reinhardt and Dieterle drew directly on the language and conventions of film. Audiences were less keen, however, and its poor box office success contributed to Reinhardt not being invited to direct any further films. Responses in England, too, were less than enthusiastic, though few so sour as that of British screen writer Sidney Carroll who dismissed the film as 'a splendiferous cinematic German-American version of *The Babes in the Woods* ... No expense has been spared with either costumes or scenery completely to eliminate Shakespeare from the picture' (quoted by Willson 2000, pp. 46–7).

Alternative Shakespeare:
Celestino Coronado (1984)

Nearly 50 years passed before *A Midsummer Night's Dream* was again filmed, when the Spanish director, Celestino Coronado, adapted Lindsay Kemp's and David Haughton's dance version, originally staged in Rome in 1979 and at Sadler's Wells, London, in 1983. Part of a wave of adaptations made by directors with an art school background and made on video or low-grade film, Coronado's work 'annexed Shakespeare for gay sensibility and the non-conformist spirit' (Howard 2007, p. 5). The text is heavily cut (the film runs to only 84 minutes), opens with a danced prologue showing Theseus' soldiers raping the Amazons, and climaxes in a performance not of *Pyramus and Thisbe*, but of *Romeo and Juliet* – on stilts. Kemp described his production (in which he played Puck) as 'a Jacobean gallimaufry, a gay fairy tale where time, order and reason have gone awry and sexual desire changes it objects in a flash' (quoted in Griffiths 1996, p. 79) and the description fits Coronado's film equally well. Titania is played as a drag queen by the blind dancer and mime Jack Birkett, otherwise known as 'The Incredible Orlando'; Oberon openly lusts after the hermaphrodite changeling boy, and though François Testory who plays the part is a young adult rather than a child, the performances do nothing to dispel the disturbing predatory nature of Oberon's sexual desires. With echoes of Titania and Penelope in the 1909 version, the young lovers desire not just other partners, but partners of their own sex: 'Demetrius rises naked from sleep to advance upon an appalled Lysander who lets his sword meekly fall and Helena and Hermia become similarly entwined' (*Guardian*, 27 April 1985), though at the film's end they all revert to their heterosexual partnerships.

Shakespeare and Hollywood 2:
Michael Hoffman (1999)

Michael Hoffman's 1999 film of *A Midsummer Night's Dream* was the first since Reinhardt's to be made in Hollywood. Hoffman transposed the action to a late-Victorian setting, and to Italy, the Villa Athena, a milieu he considered caught the 'issues of conditioning and its subversion' that he saw as central to the experiences of all the characters in the play. (Unless otherwise identified, all quotations in this section are taken from Hoffman's published script and additional notes.) The opening sequence (that recalled for many critics, as did much of Hoffman's film, Kenneth Branagh's 1993 *Much Ado About Nothing*) establishes the lavish visual style of the film. In the formal gardens and to the strains of Mendelssohn's incidental music, an army of 'servants work to line the formal garden with heavy walnut tables laid for a hundred guests' for the imminent wedding, while in the cool interior, Theseus seeks to defuse the tensions between Egeus and the young lovers. No tension exists, however, in the relationship between the Duke and Hippolyta, as the lines that underline the earlier violence between them have been cut. Indeed, comparison of script and film indicates that a scene has been cut showing Hippolyta, having argued with Theseus, at a 'desk covered with the stuff of letter writing ... on the verge of tears'. There are hints, however, of the spirit world that shadows the mortal one as during this busy preparation a gnarled boy and dwarfish woman steal from the kitchen a gramophone that reappears in Titania's bower.

Hoffman's interpretation of Bottom is distinctive. Having originally discussed with Kevin Kline, the film's star, that the actor would play Oberon, the director now wished him to play the weaver. In Hoffman's imagination, Bottom had become 'the dreamer, the actor, the pretender ... sitting at a café in a small Italian town dressed in a white suit, trying his best to look like a gentleman'. But Hoffman added more – 'that it is the only suit he owns, that he has a lousy marriage, that he lives in a dingy flat, that we know he clings to delusions of grandeur because he has no love in his life'.

The spirit world is presented as a direct mirror of the mortal one. For his inspiration for the fairies Hoffman turned to the Etruscans, as he considered 'their interest in beauty, music, magic, divination, sensuality, [...] unapologetic vanity, and their reverence for the feminine made them excellent models for the fairy world' (1999, p. 21). Hoffman filmed this fairy world in Rome's Cinecittà studios, creating a former Etruscan tomb that has been taken over as bar for a grotesque dwarves, elegant fairies, satyrs, nymphs, etc., with Puck

(Stanley Tucci) – 'a short chubby creature, hair pulled up in a topknot, head ringed in vines' – seated drinking beer. A brooding Oberon (Rupert Everett) first appears in an image drawn directly from the French painter, Gustave Moreau's sensuous *The Muses Leaving their Father Apollo* (1868), but with the painting's female Muses replaced by half-naked male fairies, while Titania (Michelle Pfeiffer), looks like a figure from a pre-Raphaelite painting, in flowing robes and carried in a luminous litter, clutching a blue-skinned changeling boy.

Unlike other films (apart from the 1909 Vitagraph version) or any stage production of which I am aware, Hoffman actually shows his audience the moment of Bottom's translation from man to ass. Bottom stands behind the hawthorn brake, waiting his cue, contemplating an elegant top hat and cane laid out (by Puck's magic) on a stump which, as Bottom tries on the hat, becomes a mirror in which he admires himself. Hearing his cue he tries to remove the hat, which, as he struggles, 'rises up to reveal a pair on enormous furry ears'. Bottom's encounter with Titania is a mix of sensual and erotic images – she awaiting him, her nakedness covered only by her long hair, he now endowed with a penis that both amazes and fascinates the fairies and their queen.

The mechanicals' play is performed in the duke's private theatre. Bottom's performance as Pyramus is grand, operatic, declamatory vocally and gesturally, whereas Flute – clumsy and breathless at rehearsal – is graceful and (within the limits of the lines she has to speak) convincing, crying over her lover's dead body and bringing tears (of sadness not mirth) to the eyes of the audience. Not only has Thisbe found truth in this fiction and been transformed into a real actor (see discussion of Supple's production, pp. 118–22), but Bottom too clearly recognises that their success is thanks to Flute's performance.

Hoffman's most significant directorial addition comes as Bottom returns alone to his flat in the village. We hear (but do not see) his wife in the background, uninterested in his experiences He stands, clasping a jewel given to him by Titania as a firefly (recalling the light that represents Tinkerbell in stage productions of *Peter Pan*) flits about in the darkness outside. (The 1935 Reinhardt-Dieterle film planned to include a wife for Bottom, but the scenes were not included in the final version; see Jackson 2007, pp. 54–5).

The Children's Midsummer Night's Dream:
Catherine Edzard (2001)

Shakespeare's plays have on numerous occasions influenced films with a direct appeal to children, such as Disney's *The Lion King* (*Hamlet*) and *Pocahontas* (*The Tempest*) or, as in the case of the Welsh-Russian co-produced *Animated Tales From Shakespeare*, provided clear and accessible versions of the plays for younger viewers. Christine Edzard's version, *The Children's 'A Midsummer Night's Dream'*, is, for me, the oddest of all screen versions of the play. Made, like her earlier film of *As You Like It* (1992), in her own tiny Sands Films Studio in London, it is the culmination of a collaboration with Southwark Education Authority to film *A Midsummer Night's Dream* with a cast and crew made up of children aged from eight to twelve from various ethnic backgrounds and drawn from local primary schools.

Edzard's basic structural concept is designed to allow her to explore the play's metatheatrical dynamics on film. The film begins with an audience of schoolchildren in a small theatre, watching a marionette version of the play, with the puppet characters voiced by experienced professional actors including Derek Jacobi and Samantha Bond. In response to Theseus' view that in distinguishing between Hermia's suitors, Demetrius 'must be held the worthier' (55), a girl in the audience stands and addresses the stage – 'I would my father looked but with my eyes' (I.i.56). From that point, the film increasingly enfolds the children into the play. They initially speak their lines while still wearing their school uniforms but are gradually absorbed into the fictional world of the play until the costumes (Elizabethan) and setting (which follows the traditional 'pictorial' approach to the design, especially the wood, with a pond to reflect the moon and a mossy floor covered with flowers) are complete. The film looks good, and many of the directorial devices are ingenious and appropriate, such as when the columns supporting the theatre's balcony sprout shoots on the way to being taken over by the forest, or having the mechanicals perform in the theatre's auditorium, now cleared of its benches, with the puppets – playing the courtly audience with their put downs to the amateur performers – being silenced by the children (a neat inversion, as Samuel Crowl points out, of the school trip to a play where the teachers do the hushing).

So far, so good, but the play is of course driven by the words the characters speak, and Shakespeare has made not inconsiderable demands on his actors through the sheer range and variety of forms of language he employs. Many adult actors, unused to Shakespeare, have struggled with the text of this play, and the child actors in Edzard's film (understandably) find it an insurmountable challenge. I have seen my own son in a school production of this play and, of course, found it admirable: but the children, like those in Edzard's film, did not – could not – bring insights to the often erotic, threatening and transforming experiences of the adult characters in the play. Crowl praises the 'innocence and charm' of Edzard's achievement, and suggests we should ignore the children's short-comings as performers and 'admire more the simple fact that they do it at all'. That sounds close to patronising to me, and though I can appreciate the experience the children involved may have had, I failed to find the adaptation as radical, exciting or illuminating of the play as others have done. (See Greenhalgh 2007 and Ford 2008 for more favourable responses to Edzard's film.)

Shakespeare on television

Extracts from *A Midsummer Night's Dream* have cropped up regularly on television (such as the Beatles performing the mechanicals' play; available on U-tube), or been used as significant elements within plays, such as in Avie Luthra's *Indian Dream* (BBC 2 October 2003), in which the performance of the play in an English village becomes a focus for Luthra's exploration of multicultural relations in modern Britain, the asylum debate and what it means to all to be 'English' (an interesting parallel with Supple's 2006 production; see Chapter 4). The first televised production of the entire play was Joan Kemp-Welch's 1964 version for Rediffusion Network Television, with Benny Hill, at the time probably the most successful and popular comedian in the country, as Bottom – a very Elizabethan casting. This was followed in 1981 by Elijah Mojinsky's production in the BBC Television Shakespeare series. The project, led by producer Cedric Messina (replaced after the second year by Jonathan Miller) with Dr John Wilders as literary consultant, was launched in 1978, with the intention of televising the 36 plays included in the First Folio over a six year period. *A Midsummer Night's*

Dream was the third of the four plays included in the fourth season, in 1981. Made entirely in BBC TV's largest studio, director Elijah Mojinsky and designer David Myerscough-Jones wanted to achieve a kind of 'romantic realism – an echo of the nineteenth century approach without its top-heaviness' (Fenwick 1981, p. 19). As if in homage to Tree's rabbits, stream and grass, they employed real horses and hounds, and two large pools of water surrounded by turf. But while everything the actors touched was to be real, the background reality of the wood was to be achieved through meshes and gauzes, 'more abstracted … and impressionistic' (Fenwick 1981, p. 19), in muted greys and browns, and dominated by a crescent moon. A similar emphasis on realism pervaded the costuming, even of the fairies (played by 30 schoolchildren) whose costumes were to be dirty from the muddy forest, and in getting the seventeenth century shape of the figures correct by paying close attention to the detail of period underwear. In fact, costumes were based around the 1630s, but not slavishly, with the characters' dress capturing what the director saw as the essence of each personality. Despite a strong cast, the result (like most of the series, with one or two notable exceptions such as Jane Howell's *Titus Andronicus*) was a staid, safe and conventional work, torn between a desire to be theatrical or televisual, and producing neither exciting Shakespeare nor exciting television.

A more radical television adaptation, shot on location, was that written by Peter Bowker for the BBC *Shakespeare Retold* series, broadcast in 2005, 'inspired by the spirit of his original plays' and designed to 'bring Shakespeare to a 21st century audience' (BBC publicity). Embracing the medium, Bowker frames his version as the viewer's dream: at the start, Puck, a magic-mushroom user in a beany hat (whose appearance reminded critics of the eco-activist Swampy, or the band Badly Drawn Boy) drops a potion in the eye of the camera, prompting a fast flash forward of (what we come to realise) are scenes to come, a tactic repeated throughout the film whenever the potion is applied. Keeping close to the basic narrative and relationships of the play, the action is re-located to a woodland Dream Park (an echo of Center Parcs), some character names are updated, and certain characters compressed or merged. A middle-aged couple, Theo and Polly, have come with their daughter Hermia and many of their and her friends (including Helena) to celebrate her engagement to James Demetrius (a rather straight, serious young man), a commitment about which she is clearly having doubts. Before the engagement is sealed, however, another youth, Zander (a good-looking, floppy haired drifter), appears to claim her, appearing soaking wet from a lake having broken in to the park (presumably with a deliberate echo of Mr Darcy emerging from the lake in the televised version of Jane Austen's *Emma*). Hermia declares she loves Zander (to Theo/Egeus's fury) and all breaks up in confusion.

The wood is inhabited by spirits, a squabbling Titania and Oberon, with Puck and other fairies, who move invisibly among the mortals. Oberon tries to solve the humans' emotional problems, while Puck (who likes 'things to get out of hand') tries to complicate them even further. Within the Park, a group of employees (under the name 'The Rude Mechanicals) are planning an entertainment for the engagement party, led by Park manager Quince and with security officer Bottom as their comic (the role played by the well-known comedian, Johnny Vegas).

Bowker largely provides a new modernised script, full of references to contemporary culture and places, but at key moments of emotional intensity the characters move into the original verse of the play. At other moments, the adaptation finds neat solutions to the essential twists in Shakespeare's plot: when Oberon instructs Puck to anoint the eyes of the 'wet' youth, for example, the confusion emerges from the pun on the physically wet Zander and the wet (drippy) Demetrius. The adaptation also glosses events in the play: coming across his wife asleep in the arms of Bottom, a complex moment (see p. 62), Oberon observes 'This is sick', while the parallel fractious relationship between Theo and Polly is resolved as they both come to realise that they've let their marriage slip, and renew their vows in the closing ceremony of the play. The final performance by 'The Rude Mechanicals', a collection of separate acts rather than a play, is heckled not by the lovers, young or old, but by a rather boorish guest, so not disturbing our sympathy for the couples. But the spirits intervene, making Snug's magic tricks actually work – to his and his audience's wonder – and, when Bottom's impressions seem doomed, transforming the act to a triumph. The film ends with Puck dropping an antidote into the camera lens/viewer's eye, and, for us too, the dream is over.

6   Critical Assessments

Although William Hazlitt firmly believed that Shakespeare's *Richard III* could 'be considered as properly a stage-play: it belongs to the theatre, rather than to the closet' (1906, p. 173), he took a diametrically opposite view of *A Midsummer Night's Dream*. This, for Hazlitt, was a play of the mind, to be read, not staged, since:

> when acted, [it] is converted into a dull pantomime. All that is finest in the play is lost in the representation, [since] Poetry and the stage do not agree well together, [and that] which was merely an airy shape, a dream, a passing thought, immediately becomes an unmanageable reality. ... Where all is left to the imagination (as in the case of reading) every circumstance, near or remote, has an equal chance of being kept in mind. ... The boards of a theatre and the regions of fancy are not the same thing. (102–3)

The first recorded assessment of *A Midsummer Night's Dream*, however, is implicitly of the play in performance, when, in 1598, two years before it appeared in print, Francis Meres observed that 'Shakespeare among the English is the most excellent in both kinds for the stage; for comedy, witness his *Gentlemen of Verona*, his *Errors*, his *Love Labours Lost*, his *Love Labours Won*, his *Midsummer's Night Dream* (sic)'. Playwrights and poets soon began to record the pleasure and inspiration they drew from the comedy (see Kennedy & Kennedy 1999, p. 4): over a hundred parallels have been identified in John Milton's work, for example, and in Joshua Poole's *English Parnassus* (1657), which offered aspiring authors models of excellence to improve their writing, *A Midsummer Night's Dream* provided 45 examples, more than any other Shakespeare play bar *Hamlet*, which supplied 48. Among the readers who also made various references to their experience of the play was King Charles I, who annotated the play in his copy of the second Folio of 1632 (which is still held in Windsor Castle).

*   *   *

To provide even a survey of subsequent critical approaches to the play is not possible in one short chapter. However, throughout the play's long life, certain aspects of it have recurred in much of the critical writing (as well as preoccupying those who have presented it on stage and screen), and I have used these topics to structure the following highly selective discussion.

Fairies and magic

Granville Barker, who directed the play in 1914 (see Chapter 4, pp. 110–14) observed that the fairies are any director's biggest headache, and they absorb the attention of critics just as actively, who ponder their origins, their relationship to the play as a whole and the viability of presenting such creatures on stage. Indeed, the first sustained writing on the play, John Dryden's preface to his never-performed, opera-cum-play, *The State of Innocence* (1677), a version of *Paradise Lost*, sees him defending Shakespeare's representation of a fairy world in the context of late seventeenth century determinism, arguing that 'Poets may be allowed the … liberty, for describing things which exist not, if they are founded on popular belief: of this nature are fairies, pygmies, and the extraordinary effects of magic: for 'tis still an imitation, though of other men's fancies.' The fairy world continued to be a focus of interest. In 1709, Nicholas Rowe, the first editor of Shakespeare, wrote in the introduction to his edition that 'certainly the greatness of this author's genius does nowhere so much appear, as where he gives his imagination an entire loose, and raises his fancy to a flight above mankind and the limits of the visible world', and Rowe chose an image representing the encounter of Oberon and Titania in II.i to illustrate the play. Dryden's argument that the portrayal of fairies was justified by contemporary belief continued to be advanced. In 1712, Joseph Addison in the influential *Spectator* praised Shakespeare for making the fairies appear so 'natural', that 'though we have no rule by which to judge them … if there are such beings in the world, it looks highly probable they should talk and act as he has presented them'. Throughout the eighteenth century critics also continued to admire Shakespeare's powers of creative imagination that enabled him to represent the supernatural world and its inhabitants: Francis Gentleman, for example, wrote in the Bell edition of 1774 that Shakespeare 'had an inexhaustible fund of fancy for supernatural beings', giving them 'language peculiarly and happily suited to themselves'.

From the eighteenth century on, artists found the play a particular productive subject, often drawing out the darker, sometimes erotic undercurrents of the play not touched on in written criticism or found in productions, such as in Henry Fuseli's 'Titania Embracing Bottom' (1792) or his earlier, related painting 'The Nightmare' (c. 1782), David Scott's 'Puck Fleeing from the Dawn', 1837, or Joseph Paton's 'The Fairy Raid' (see Commentary, p. 60). In his essay, 'A *Midsummer Night's Dream*: A Visual Re-Creation' – a rare exploration of the relationship between how artists represent the play and its critical and theatrical history – W. Moelwyn Merchant reveals the play as portraying 'a life altogether darker than the apparent grace of the fairy world' (1961, p. 165; see also Stanley Wells, *Shakespeare For All Time*, Basingstoke: Macmillan, 2002).

The physical nature of the fairies, and the related issue of how to represent them on stage, especially with adult actors, troubled Hazlitt – 'Fairies are not incredible, but fairies six foot high are so' – and George Daniel imagined Shakespeare creating them, with 'his pencil … dipped in the dews of heaven' but again, producing fairies 'too airy … to be represented by the sons of dull earth' (1828). Considering the historical 'evidence', Frank Sidgewick (1908) thought Shakespeare had miniaturized the fairies (Kennedy & Kennedy 1999, pp. 102, 370). Minor White Latham (1930), in a major study, suggested Shakespeare was an innovator not only in presenting the fairies as small (though earlier examples have since been found), but also in presenting them as friendly to human beings. Both views were subsequently contested: Katherine Briggs argued for contemporary belief pre-dating the play that fairies were small (1959) and Keith Thomas noted that 'fairies might reward benefactors, but if neglected would avenge' (Thomas 1973, p. 728).

Augustine Skottowe's description of the fairies as gossamer creatures moving 'amidst the fragrance of enamelled meads, graceful, lovely and enchanting' (1824) (Kennedy & Kennedy 1999, p. 100) is typical of a longstanding and widely held view that has helped create the impression of the play as 'the school-play Shakespeare *par excellence*' (Holland 1994, p. 73) reflected in stage productions throughout the nineteenth and, indeed (though increasingly rarely) twentieth century, as well as in critical commentaries. Dover Wilson, for example, in *Shakespeare's Happy Comedies* (1962), summed up the play as embodying 'innocence, lyricism, poetic beauty, universal love', a view endorsed ten years later by Thomas McFarland, for whom the play, 'the happiest of Shakespeare's plays', represents an 'extended arabesque of hope and joy' (1972, pp. 78, 97).

Others, like the painters referred to above, have found more sombre aspects to the play and its portrayal of the spirit world In 1856, William Watkiss Lloyd noted that 'in psychology, the assumption of fairy or other supernatural influence is a suggestion of incidents that bear characteristics of passion, without the intervention of human or other observable passionate agents' (Kennedy & Kennedy 1999, p.199), while other nineteenth century critics focused on the fairies and their magic as being 'without delicate feeling and without morality' as they 'tempt mortals to infidelity'. Georg Brandes, the Danish writer and scholar, anticipated twentieth century critical views that found a psycho-sexual subtext to the play, often closely linked to its 'dream' quality. He argued that 'Oberon's magic is simply a great symbol typifying the sorcery of the erotic imagination' and that Shakespeare 'felt and divined how much wider is the domain of the unconscious than of the conscious life, and saw that our moods and passions have their root in the unconscious' (quoted in Kehler 1998, p. 11). In 1932 G. Wilson Knight wrote of 'a gnomish, fearsome, *Macbeth*-like quality' to the play (p. 69), while George A. Bonnard (1956) saw the fairies as lacking 'all sense of responsibility, all moral impulse' (Kehler 1998, p. 25). Especially influential in challenging the 'gossamer' view of the play was an essay by the Polish critic, Jan Kott, included in a book first published in 1961 and which appeared in English under the title *Shakespeare Our Contemporary* in 1965. For Kott, 'The *Dream* is the most erotic of Shakespeare's plays', but he argues that in none of Shakespeare's other works (except *Troilus and Cressida*) 'is the eroticism expressed so brutally' (1983, p. 175). Kott argues that the 'metaphors of love, eroticism and sex' (p. 179) are at first completely traditional (Cupid, roses, etc) but that the play and its lovers move into 'the dark sphere of animal love-making' in a forest inhabited not just by fairies but by beasts that 'represent abundant sexual potency' (p. 182). Kott's vision of those fairies is about as far from Tree's flying children as possible (and not immediately obvious from the text): 'I imagine Titania's court as consisting of old men and women, toothless and shaking, their mouths wet with saliva, who sniggeringly procure a monster for their mistress' (p. 182), and he turned to the eighteenth century Spanish painter, Goya, and to his *Los Caprichos* etchings in particular, for a visual analogue (see Robert Hughes, *Goya*, 2003, pp. 177–215). Although Kott was not (as some believe) the first critic to assert that Titania and Bottom (as the ass) had intercourse together, his essay contributed directly to a shift in the representation of the event on stage, notably in productions by John Hancock and Peter Brook, staged in San Francisco and Stratford-upon-Avon respectively shortly after Kott's book appeared. To readers today, however, Kott's use of racial and sexual stereotypes – out of date even in his own time – is to us unacceptable. For example, to illuminate his idea of the bizarre sexual congress between fairy and ass, spirit and mortal, he compares Titania in the ass's embrace to 'the white Scandinavian girls I used to see … walking and clinging tightly to Negroes with faces grey or so black that they were almost indistinguishable from the night' (Kott 1965, p. 183). Kott's (and Brook's) response to the play was echoed by critics such as Hugh Richmond, who (rather peculiarly) compared Titania's 'grotesque passion' for Bottom/the ass to the 'sadomasochistic type of sexuality' of Helena and Demetrius, but it also produced some strenuous opposition. Michael MacOwan, unable to resist his own prejudice ('how good is [Kott's] English, I wonder?'), responded:

> Kott relies on bald, repetitive assertion rather than logical reasoning: he ignores or distorts opinions opposite to his own; he constantly manipulates facts to suit theories and colours his whole book with a pervasive, gloating salacity sometimes on the edge of hysteria. (quoted by Kehler 1998, p. 30)

A more balanced response came from David Bevington, who found Kott's stress on the fractures brought about by sexual betrayal and rivalry 'helpful … though he has surely gone too far' (1975, p. 86). In a recent, brilliant essay, A. D. Nuttall argues that 'the whole point' of the play is its 'gossamer beauty', but that twentieth century criticism has been 'marked by a prejudice in favour of the discordant', and that nowhere is that prejudice more evident than in Jan Kott:

> His notorious description of Titania as 'longing for animal love' (as if Titania were Pasiphae) is simply ludicrous. Has he not noticed that Titania is deluded? She is attracted by what she sees as a wise and beautiful being. She cannot see the grotesque half-donkey available to the rest of us. (2000, p. 51)

While acknowledging that Theseus was a ravisher of women, Nuttall argues that what happens in Theseus' 'wholly benevolent speech to Hippolyta [in the opening scene] is a *successful* banishing of the old dark narrative from the play. With these words the myth is turned on its head; the harsh Theseus drops out of sight and the smiling Duke of Athens springs up in its place' (p. 51), to create 'another story, one (why should we be so reluctant to receive it?) of happy love' (p. 52). Now, not everyone (including me) agrees with that reading, of either the opening exchanges or of Theseus' and Hippolyta's relationship overall (see Commentary, *passim*). Nor for that matter does Nuttall – at least, not entirely. Working with the concept of *apotrope* as used by Richard Wilson in his essay, 'The Kindly Ones: The Death of the Author in Shakespearean Athens', and drawing too on Peter Holland's 'Theseus' Shadows in *A Midsummer Night's Dream*', Nuttall argues that with all the elements of the play – court, fairies and workers – Shakespeare, while essentially writing a happy comedy, is careful to ensure that a 'darker penumbra of meaning' is still present. So far as the Bottom–Titania relationship is concerned, in which 'ancient stories of bestial coupling remain relevant' (p. 55) – including, of course, the Theseus-related myth of Pasiphae and the Minotaur – he writes:

> Having asserted the comic innocence of Bottom, I must acknowledge that the mere sight of a woman entwined with a beast or half-beast of itself suggests monstrosity. Again, I have to ask, are the demons completely removed? Is our laughter simple, unmixed, or is it the louder because energized by a surviving anxiety? (p. 55)

For Nuttall it is the latter: 'As the Plutarchian Theseus stands behind the Duke of Athens, so the Golden Ass of Lucius Apuleius stands behind Bottom the Weaver' (p. 56). The play, he concludes, therefore:

> entails a negotiation – with a long spoon, as it were – between comedy and tragedy, between comedy and myth, a negotiation, that is, between joy and fear, resulting in an *apotrope* of the latter. Just that, *apotrope*, not abolition. (p. 59)

I have dwelt on Nuttall's essay because (without actually mentioning it) it grasps that *A Midsummer Night's Dream* (like so much of Shakespeare's and his contemporaries' work) sits within the tradition of the grotesque, a concept that embraces the simultaneous presence of contradictory, contrasting elements, and an idea that seems to me to be fundamental to any reading or production of this play. Nuttall sees the balance between the comic and serious as about 90% the former, 10% the latter – other readings, my own included, would move those somewhat closer together (see p. 85).

Sex, gender and power

The publication in 1985 of a collection of new essays under the title *Political Shakespeare* was representative of a change in critical preoccupations around Shakespeare's work that, in the Marxist tradition, saw a play as a reflection of its contemporary social and political context (see the essay by Krieger in Further Reading, for an example) or pursued a New Historicist approach that viewed literature as one of the ways in which that context is itself constructed. Leonard Tennenhouse's essay in the volume focuses on the relationships in *A Midsummer Night's Dream* between fathers and children and ruler and subject. Juxtaposing Theseus and Oberon ('the traditional alternative to patriarchal law', p. 111), and the play and the later masque by Ben Jonson, *Oberon*, Tennenhouse interprets *A Midsummer Night's Dream* in the context of Elizabethan power relations between monarch and people: 'the entire last act of the play consequently theorises the process of inversion whereby art and politics end up in this mutually authorising relationship' (1985, p. 112).

The collision of female will with male power, and the apparent suppression of women within the play has provided a focus for what would later become defined as feminist criticism. This has not been entirely the prerogative of the late twentieth century. In 1895, for example, an American teacher and scholar, Katharine Lee Bates, published an edition of *A Midsummer Night's Dream*, in which she wryly observed of the relationship between Theseus and Hippolyta that while the Amazon queen 'has dignity of silence, grace of speech, but little ardor, mirth or power of personality ... Theseus is too evidently her conqueror. Even in trifles the man must have his way, and the woman must accept his assurance that she likes it better than her own' (quoted in Kennedy & Kennedy 1999, p. 322). Although, as Dutton points out (1996, p. 97), *A Midsummer Night's Dream* has received less attention from feminist critics than other plays, it has opened up significant perspectives on the play. Shirley Nelson Garner, for example, sees the play as exploring male suppression of the female characters, affirming 'patriarchal order and hierarchy [and] insisting that the power of women must be circumscribed' (1981, pp. 47, 84). More recently, in her acute introduction to the new Penguin edition, Helen Hackett observes of the ambivalent use of moon/virgin imagery in the period, and in this play in particular:

> The narrative movement of Shakespeare's play, from unnatural chaos brought on by the assertion of female power, to order restored by the conversion of all the women into compliant wives, suggests a great deal about what [Shakespeare] thought of female rule. (2005, p. xlvii)

Studying *A Midsummer Night's Dream* it's impossible not to encounter Louis A. Montrose's essay, 'Figurations of Gender and Power', which first appeared in the first issue of the New Historicist journal, *Representations*, and has appeared in various forms since. One of an influential series by Montrose on the place of Shakespeare's texts in the cultural and power-relations of Elizabethan England, it examines the complex inter-textuality of the play. Focusing on systems of gender and nurture within a 'patriarchal norm', Montrose explores how 'While Shakespeare's plays reproduce these legitimizing structures, they also reproduce challenges to their legitimacy' (pp. 109, 117; quotations are from Dutton 1996). For example, of the exchanges between Theseus, Egeus and Hermia in the opening scene he writes:

> Theseus has characteristically Protestant notions about the virtue of virginity: maidenhood is a phase in the life-cycle of a woman who is destined for married chastity and motherhood. As a permanent state,

'single blessedness' is mere sterility. Theseus expands Hermia's options only in order to clarify the constraints. In the process of tempering the father's domestic tyranny, the Duke affirms his own interests and authority. He represents the life of a vestal as a *punishment*, and it is one that fits the nature of Hermia's crime. The maiden is surrounded by men, each of whom – as father, lover, or lord – claims a kind of property in her. Yet Hermia dares to suggest she has a claim to property in herself. ... The self-possession of single blessedness is a form of power against which are opposed the marriage doctrines of Shakespeare's culture and the very form of his comedy. (p. 109)

Sexualities

The iconic image of Titania and Bottom, lovingly entwined, has been the focal point of much critical writing on the play (see above), and treated very differently across stage productions. The question of whether they actually have sexual intercourse has been one preoccupation (James L. Calderwood has conveniently summed up the thinking on both sides on that one, while it receives a witty discussion in Sutherland & Watts 2000, pp. 137–42); another key question has been to consider how we might read this bizarre coupling in terms of the play overall.

In 1837, William Maginn offered an explanation of Titania's infatuation with Bottom by comparing it to everyday experience of 'ill-mated loves':

Many is the Titania driven by some unintelligible magic so to waste her love. Some juice, potent as that of Puck ... often converts in the eyes of woman the grossest defects into resistless charms. (Kennedy & Kennedy 1999, p. 115)

In 1856, William Watkiss Lloyd, considered other forms of ill-mating, wondering in passing whether Bottom's ass-head and Puck as a headless bear might 'indicate the popular currency of some milder form of lycanthropy' (Kennedy & Kennedy 1999, p. 198), but ultimately interpreting the mis-match in terms of the social hierarchy, quoting from Henry Fielding's *Tom Thumb*: Love 'Lords into cellars bears, / And bids the brawny porter walk upstairs' (II.v.11–12). Recently, however, critics have begun to examine more closely the implications of the cross-species nature of the liaison, with some linking it to 'the plays language of patriarchal hegemony'

(Boehrer 2004, p. 99). Other critics have located in the moment a mother/child relationship simultaneously with the more erotic one already discussed, one that resonates with Titania's childless state: 'Through the substitution of Bottom for the changeling in Titania's arms, the forest episodes stage the absurd-yet-compelling fantasy of a return to a female-dominated space of magic and beauty' (Lamb 2000, p. 305).

Critics have also explored the significance of human same-sex relationships in the play: for example, Kathryn Schwarz offers a detailed reading of the play in the light of homo-social attachments, male and female (2000, pp. 204–35), Louis Montrose notes the extent to which, in the fairy plot-line, 'the relationship between women' displaces that 'between wife and husband' (1996, p. 139), and Gail Paster and Skiles Howard focus on the attachment between Hermia and Helena, which 'as the male-female couples move inexorably towards marriage' is 'gradually erased' (1999, pp. 193–4). Douglas E. Green's essay, 'Preposterous Pleasures: Queer Theories and *A Midsummer Night's Dream*' (in Kehler 1998, pp. 369–97) seeks to explore some of the play's male and female '"homoerotic significations"', which the author sees as its 'moments of "queer disruption" and eruption' (p. 370). Green acknowledges that the 'isolated "queer" moments' he identifies result from pursuing Walter Benjamin's advice to read consciously and conscientiously 'against the grain of the text' (p. 381). Alan Sinfield also adopts this approach:

> Myself, I find the patriarchal figures in *A Midsummer Night's Dream* oppressive, and the same-sex relations to be the most vigorous and moving parts. ... To get what I regard as a happy ending I would show the boys and girls successfully resisting the effect of Oberon's drugs, and producing some more interpersonal combinations. However, it is hard to see Theseus and Oberon permitting that. Perhaps the more effective move would be to disclose the tragedy in the conventional ending. This would involve presenting the boys and girls as manifestly brainwashed and infantilized by Puck's manipulations of their minds and bodies into heterosexual pairings. (Sinfield 2003, pp. 76–7)

Dreams

Only a few fragments survive of Samuel Taylor Coleridge's comments on the play: a lecture delivered on 19 December 1811 has not survived, and the one advertised for Bristol in the 1813–14 series was evidently never given. However, his note in his copy of Theobald's 1773 edition, that 'Shakespeare availed himself of the title of this play in his own mind, and worked on it as a dream throughout' signalled an interest that was to preoccupy later critics, some seeing the play's representation of a dream as a key to the play's structure, others approaching it through a psychoanalytic analysis. Weston A. Gui (1952) was one of the first to pursue the latter approach, seeing Bottom's dream as really Shakespeare's, with the absent Indian boy being the playwright's younger brother whom he displaces. Gerald F. Jacobson (1962) also homed in on the changeling as 'the little girl's fantasy of stealing mother's baby, and killing mother, as in this case the stolen child belonged to a woman who died in childbirth' (Kehler 1998, p. 39). Two essays in particular are valuable in this area: Norman Holland's 1979 essay, 'Hermia's Dream' (reprinted in Dutton 1996, pp. 61–83), and Barbara Freedman's 'Dis/Figuring Power: Censorship and Representation in *A Midsummer Night's Dream*' (1991; Kehler 1998, pp. 179–215).

Structure

In 1904, G. K. Chesterton wrote that 'the supreme literary merit of *A Midsummer Night's Dream* is a merit of design', and many who write on the play are similarly admiring. However, those who sought to 'improve' Shakespeare in the years following the reopening of the playhouses, or to meet the demands of contemporary taste, frequently criticised what they perceive as his failure to control his material, considering the play's extraordinary 'beauties' (of language, most usually) to be set within an inferior structure. Two key contributions from the first half of the nineteenth century signalled a shift in critical approaches to the form of *A Midsummer Night's Dream*: the German critic Augustus Schlegel's 1815 lecture, 'Criticisms on Shakespeare's Comedies', and J. O. Halliwell's *An Introduction to Shakespeare's Midsummer Night's Dream* (1841), the first book-length study devoted to the play. Schlegel attempted (really for the first time in any systematic way) to analyse the interrelationship of the play's language and shifting verse forms, its mixed tones, and the interdependence of the different worlds, character groups and events:

> *A Midsummer Night's Dream* and *The Tempest* may be in so far compared together that in both the influence of a wonderful world of spirits is

interwoven with the turmoil of human passion and with the farcical adventures of folly.... The different parts of the plot; the wedding of Theseus and Hippolyta, Oberon and Titania's quarrel, the flight of the two pairs of lovers, and the theatrical manoeuvres of the mechanics are so lightly interwoven that they seem necessary to each other for the formation of a whole.... The extremes of fanciful and vulgar are united when the enchanted Titania awakes and falls in love with a coarse mechanic with an ass's head, who represents, or rather disfigures, the part of a tragical lover.... Pyramus and Thisbe is not unmeaningly chosen as the grotesque play within the play; it is exactly like the pathetic part of the piece, a secret meeting of two lovers in the forest, and their separation by an unfortunate accident, and closes the whole with the most amusing parody. (1846, pp. 393–4)

Halliwell (more often referred to now as Halliwell-Phillipps, after he added his wife's name to his own in 1874) went further. He commented on previous criticism, scrutinised the play's time-structure and other 'inconsistencies' (which he argued did not 'detract from the most beautiful poetic drama in this or any other language'), considered possible sources (offering for the first time a ballad of Ovid's story of Midas from *Metamorphoses* as a source for Bottom's transformation) and challenged the play's 'alleged unfitness' for the stage, using the then-current production at Covent Garden, starring Madame Vestris, as his example of its potential to succeed in the theatre (see pp. 104–5). In 1874, Denton Jacques Snider published an essay aimed at challenging those who 'regard any attempt to make out a consistent unity in [*A Midsummer Night's Dream*] as wanton and absurd refinement'. He saw three divisions in the play: the Real World, the Fairy World and the Representation of Art. In this last part, he explains: 'The first two parts mirror themselves, the action reflects itself, the play plays itself playing, it is its own spectator, including its audience and itself in one and the same movement. Thus there is reached a totality of Representation which not only represents something, but represents itself in the act of Representation' (Kennedy & Kennedy 1999, p. 246). We would call the structure Snider is describing 'metatheatrical' or 'self-reflexive', a concept most fully expounded in Lionel Abel's pioneering study *Metatheatre: a new view of dramatic form* (1963). It is a defining characteristic of early modern drama in general, but absolutely central to an understanding of this particular play. Two later studies in particular have explored this key aspect of the play: James L. Calderwood's *Shakespearean Metadrama* (1971) and Anne Righter (Barton)'s seminal book, *Shakespeare and the Idea of the Play* (1962), which although it touches only briefly on *A Midsummer Night's Dream* constantly raises ideas that illuminate the play.

Language

The earliest known critic of the play, Francis Meres, praised Shakespeare's 'mellifluous', 'honey-tongued' dramatic voice, and all who have subsequently focused on the play's language are generally in agreement with Christy Desmet (who approaches the play's rhetoric from a feminist perspective):

> In this play, Shakespeare has compiled a rich anthology of poetic styles, ranging from the Petrarchan exchanges of the young lovers through the Senecan bombast of 'Pyramus and Thisbe' to Puck's racing couplets and the unnamed fairy's lilting triplets. (Kehler 1998, p. 297)

Although some early commentators were critical of what they saw as excessiveness in Shakespeare's dramatic poetry, the majority praised what they termed its 'Beauties' (even those, such as the editor Charles Gildon, who thought they were buried in plays he dismissed as 'a heap of rubbish'). Alexander Pope, for example, in his edition (1723–5) marked in the text what he considered 'the most shining passages', and other editors followed suit, culminating in William Dodd's *Beauties of Shakespeare*, which was first published in 1752, but was regularly reissued until 1903. The impact of this selective approach (as with Charles Lamb's 1813 collection, *Specimens of Specimens of English dramatic poets who lived about the time of Shakespeare*) is to focus on parts of a play that are deemed to be good (i.e., those which meet contemporary tastes) rather than considering it as a whole, a process not dissimilar to the play's treatment on stage, where those parts that offended contemporary critical taste were omitted or, to recall Davenant's term, 'regularized'.

Two books published in the 1930s explored the play's imagery. G. Wilson Knight identified the sometimes sinister implications of that imagery in *The Shakespearean Tempest* (1932), observing – as had Victorian painters and as later critics would – that the play 'continually suggests a nightmare terror' (p. 146). In Caroline Spurgeon's ground-breaking book, *Shakespeare's Imagery and What It Tells Us* (1935) she examined the way imagery creates atmosphere and background and steers, at times subliminally, our response to a play.

However, critics disagree 'about the effect of Shakespeare's verbal pyrotechnics', with some perceiving 'a discrepancy between poetic sound and sense that subverts the play's claims for the healing power of imagination', while others discern 'an authentic, redemptive voice beneath the artificial rhetoric and undisciplined brawling that dominates for most of the play' (Desmet 1998, p. 297) .

Throughout the Commentary I have noted the sheer range and variety of Shakespeare's use of language, the care he takes in giving each group of characters its own linguistic register, so that the play's 'triple structure is reproduced stylistically by the differences between the verse of the nobles and that of the fairies, and by the use of prose for the rustics' (Vickers 1968, p. 65). Theseus and Hippolyta speak in regular iambic pentameter blank verse, moving into prose to interrupt the performance of *Pyramus and Thisbe*. Oberon and Titania speak blank verse too, but also speak decasyllabic, rhyming couplets, while Oberon delivers his magic spells in seven syllable trochaics. The other fairies also speak in couplets, and in rhymed short verse, the lovers in blank verse and couplets. The mechanicals speak predominantly in prose but also, when acting, deliver a variety of verse forms. Vickers observes that Shakespeare's audience could register these stylistic shifts and collisions in a way we probably cannot, noting that they are 'determined by larger dramatic functions' (1968, pp. 6, 248).

I have also tried to indicate how, far from being merely a display of his technical virtuosity, these rhetorical skills are key to his articulation of the play's 'meanings'. Critics who have focused to different degrees on the language include David Young (1966), Stephen Fender (1968) and R. A. Foakes in his excellent introduction to the New Cambridge edition (1984; updated 2003).

Taking a political and historical, multilingual and interlingual approach to Shakespeare's language, Patricia Parker attends as closely as anyone to the words, and encourages us to do the same, in, for example, *Shakespeare from the Margins: Language, Culture, Context* (1996), and in her contribution to the Fifth Wall Symposium in London in 2004, where, locating language as a political act, she commented that:

> The attempt to 'govern' sound was … just beginning for English itself in Shakespeare's day – through the new disciplines in England of grammar and punctuation and the beginnings of the standardisation of spellings, that would yield (only much later) different accepted spellings for words whose meaning was different, though their sounds were the same. It seems to me that *A Midsummer Night's Dream* stages some of these contemporary tensions between the new (elite) humanist disciplines of grammar and more oral (and less literate) modes – in the snide and often pedantic remarks of the aristocrats [when they ridicule] the artisans in the final scene … When Hippolyta remarks in response to Quince's mis-punctuated Prologue … that it is 'sound', but not in 'government', I think that the line itself gives us an insight into the connections in the period between governing sounds and other kinds of sound government. (2005, p. 126)

Frank Kermode, tracing Shakespeare's language chronologically through his work, observes that, in *A Midsummer Night's Dream*, 'We are approaching the time when Shakespeare began to use a word or group of words as a central element, almost as a subject of exploration in his verse' (2000, p. 59). Kermode offers as an example Shakespeare's repeated use of the verb 'to dote', and concludes his discussion:

> One of [the play's] characteristics [is] the bursting through into the action of what seems a merely verbal trick. Here it is the insistent talk of eyes, the patterns of blindness and insight, wood and city, phantasma and vision, love vulgar and love celestial. The juices of love-in-idleness and of 'Dian's bud' are there as complements to the talk of eyes and sight; Bottom's dream as the complement or opposite of the rationality of a prince of the world. Word and action go together, and the word must be closely attended to. (64)

Performance

Kermode's insistence, like Hamlet's, on the link between word and action brings me finally to performance-centred criticism. Harley Granville Barker's *Prefaces to Shakespeare* are essential reading. He published his first, brief *Preface* to *A Midsummer Night's Dream* following his 1914 production (see pp. 110–14), and a second, fuller version followed in 1924. Both are full of revealing insights to the play in performance: as he wrote, 'We have the text to guide us, half a dozen stage directions, and that is all. I abide by the text and the demands of the text and beyond that I claim freedom' (p. vi). A stage-focused approach to the study of Shakespeare was developed more extensively during the 1960s and 1970s by critics such as J. L. Styan, Bernard Beckerman, Glynne Wickham, John Russell Brown and Peter Thomson, that sought to reveal the vocal and physical languages of the plays and their interaction with performance space, sometimes (but not always) tying these textual discussions to a growing sense of the early modern playhouses (as, for example, Wickham does in his chapter 'A *Midsummer Night's Dream*: the Setting and the Text' in *Shakespeare's Dramatic Heritage* (1969). The value of drawing together textual and performance issues is seen, for example, in Barbara Hodgdon's exploration of the implications of Egeus' absence from Act V in the quarto versus his presence in Act V in the Folio (which she sees as possibly revealing Shakespeare's 'revising mind', and Philip McGuire's examination of the impact of Hippolyta's silence in Act I and Egeus' in Act IV (both essays are reprinted in Dutton 1996). John Russell Brown, from his early *Shakespeare's Plays in Performance* (1966) to his recent *Shakespeare Dancing: a Theatrical Study of the Plays* (2005) has advocated a critical approach to Shakespeare that, as do this series of Handbooks, seeks to explore Shakespeare's verbal *and* physical imagination and how they are embodied in the act of performance. While acknowledging that the 'words of a text are vital elements in the performance of Shakespeare's plays', he offers a slight corrective to an over-concentration on language: 'Physical enactment in time and space, and not the speaking of the texts, is the element for which Shakespeare wrote and in which his plays were to live' (Brown 2005, p. vii).

This brief survey can do no more than sketch in the shape of the landscape of critical responses to the play. Further guidance on trends, and examples of key texts, can be found in the collections of essays listed in Further Reading, where you can also find full details of the works discussed here, and others that I recommend.

Further Reading

Editions of the play – introductions

John F. Andrews (ed.), *The Everyman Shakespeare* (London: J. M. Dent, 1993). Notes and glossary are set out on a page facing the page of text. I found its notes often picked up details of interpretation not commented on in other editions.

Harold F. Brooks (ed.), *The Arden Shakespeare*, Third Series (London: Methuen, 1979). Brooks, who has the distinction of having seen Granville Barker's 1914 production, provides a clear scholarly introduction, divided into topics, and extensive examples of source materials.

R. A. Foakes (ed.), *New Cambridge Shakespeare* (Cambridge: Cambridge University Press, updated edition, 2003). Foakes' introduction is totally alert to the text and its possibilities in performance, and includes a well-illustrated stage history. Highly recommended.

Trevor R. Griffiths, *Shakespeare in Production: A Midsummer Night's Dream* (Cambridge: Cambridge University Press, 1996). An indispensible study of the play on stage.

Peter Holland (ed.), *The Oxford Shakespeare* (Oxford: Oxford University Press, 1994). A very thorough introduction (though some have criticised his adherence to Freudian dream-theory) that is distinctive in absorbing the play's stage history and life into the general discussion.

Stanley Wells (ed.), *The New Penguin Shakespeare* (London: Penguin Books, 1967). Much used in production as the notes are confined to the back, leaving only the text on the page. Wells' introduction is alert to the moment by moment shifts of the play in performance. The edition was reissued in 2005 with Wells' text and commentary but with a new Introduction and a chronology of Shakespeare's plays by Helen Hackett that offers a more feminist interpretation of the play.

Critical histories and anthologies

Richard Dutton (ed.), *A Midsummer Night's Dream*, New Casebook series (Basingstoke: Macmillan, 1996). An excellent Introduction usefully explores trends in criticism of the play in the second half of the twentieth century and includes representative examples.

Dorothea Kehler (ed.), *A Midsummer Night's Dream: Critical Essays* (New York & London: Garland, 1998). A lengthy Introduction, subdivided into topics, is followed by a good range of critical writing, some written especially for this volume, and including, in a final section, reviews of the play on stage.

Judith M. Kennedy and Richard F. Kennedy (eds), *Shakespeare: The Critical Tradition – A Midsummer Night's Dream* (London & New Brunswick, NJ: Athlone Press, 1999). Indispensible; the Introduction discusses work up until the 1980s, but the extracts stop in 1920.

Antony Price (ed.), *A Midsummer Night's Dream*, Casebook series (Basingstoke: Macmillan, 1983). The precursor to Dutton's volume (see above) Price reprints critical studies between 1930 and 1974, but refers also to earlier critical readings and productions.

Emma Smith (ed.), *Shakespeare's Comedies* (London: Blackwell, 2004). The volume looks at its subject from different critical perspectives, and has a useful introductory essay by Smith, 'The Development of Criticism of Shakespeare's Comedies'. There is one essay devoted to *A Midsummer Night's Dream*.

Critical assessments

F. Murray Abraham, *Actors on Shakespeare: A Midsummer Night's Dream* (London: Faber and Faber, 2005).

Robert Hamilton Ball, *Shakespeare on Silent Film: A Strange Eventful History* (London: George Allen and Unwin, Ltd., 1968). An extremely detailed and valuable study.

C. L. Barber, *Shakespeare's Festive Comedy: A Study of Dramatic Form and Its Relation to Social Customs* (Princeton NJ: Princeton University Press, 1959).

Harley Granville Barker, *Prefaces to Shakespeare: A Midsummer Night's Dream*: originally published 1914, second version 1924 (London: Nick Hern Books, 1993).

Jonathan Bate, *The Genius of Shakespeare* (Basingstoke: Macmillan, 1997).

Catherine Belsey, 'A *Midsummer Night's Dream*: a modern perspective', in Barbara A. Mowat and Paul Werstine (eds), *A Midsummer Night's Dream* (New York: Washington Square Press, 1993).

David Bevington, '"But We Are Spirits of Another Sort": The Dark Side of Love and Magic', *A Midsummer Night's Dream*', *Medieval and Renaissance Studies*, 7 (1975), 80–92. (Reprinted in Dutton 1996, 24–37.)

Harold Bloom, *Shakespeare: The Invention of the Human* (London: Fourth Estate, 1999).

Bruce Boehrer, 'Economies of Desire in *A Midsummer Night's Dream*', *Shakespeare Studies*, XXXII (2004), 99–117.

Michael Bristol, *Carnival and Theatre: Plebeian Culture and the Structure of Authority in Early Modern England* (London: Methuen, 1985).

Douglas Brode, *Shakespeare in the Movies: from the Silent Era to Shakespeare in Love* (Oxford: Oxford University Press, 2000). A wide-ranging survey.

John Russell Brown, *Shakespeare's Plays in Performance* (London: Edward Arnold, 1966).

John Russell Brown, *Shakespeare Dancing: A Theatrical Study of the Plays* (Basingstoke: Palgrave Macmillan, 2005).

Judith Buchanan, *Shakespeare on Film* (Harlow: Pearson Longman, 2005). A very thorough, imaginative and stimulating study.

Stephen M. Buhler, *Shakespeare in the Cinema* (Albany: State University of New York, 2002).

Mark Thornton Burnett, *Filming Shakespeare in the Global Marketplace* (Basingstoke: Palgrave Macmillan, 2007). Chapter 2, 'Sequelizing Shakespeare' focuses on relationships between Hoffman's *A Midsummer Night's Dream* and Kenneth Branagh's film of *Much Ado About Nothing* (1993).

Mark Thornton Burnett and Ramona Wray, *Screening Shakespeare in the Twenty-First Century* (Edinburgh: Edinburgh University Press, 2006). Contains rare analysis of Luthra's *Indian Dream* and Cates' *A Midsummer Night's Rave*.

Richard Burt and Lynda E. Boose (eds), *Shakespeare the Movie II: Popularising the Plays on Film, Tv, Video, and Dvd* (London: Routledge, 2003).

James L. Calderwood, *A Midsummer Night's Dream: Harvester New Critical Introductions to Shakespeare* (Hemel Hempsted: Harvester Wheatsheaf, 1992). One of my favourite books on the play, it is beautifully written with a host of perceptive observations, often on small, easily overlooked details. Contains a brief but useful survey of critical approaches (pp. xx–xxvi).

William C. Carroll, *The Metamorphoses of Shakespearean Comedy* (Princeton: Princeton University Press, 1985), especially pp. 141–77.

J. P. Conlan, 'The Fey Beauty of *A Midsummer Night's Dream*: A Shakespearean Comedy in its Courtly Context', *Shakespeare Studies*, 32 (2004), 118–72.

Samuel Crowl, *Shakespeare at the Cineplex* (Athens: Ohio University Press, 2003). A lively study of Shakespeare films that emerged in the last decade or so of the twentieth century, including those of *A Midsummer Night's Dream* directed by Hoffman, Noble – and, in more detail – Edzard.

Clifford Davidson, '"What hempen home-spuns have we swaggering here?" Amateur Actors in *A Midsummer Night's Dream* and the Coventry Civic Plays and Pageants', *Shakespeare Studies*, 19 (1987), 87–99.

Christy Desmet, 'Disfiguring Women with Masculine Tropes: A Rhetorical Reading of *A Midsummer Night's Dream*' in Kehler 1998, 299–329.

Alan C. Dessen and Leslie Thomson, *A Dictionary of Stage Directions in English Drama, 1580–1642* (Cambridge: Cambridge University Press, 1999).

Michael Dobson, 'Shakespeare as a Joke: the English Comic Tradition, *A Midsummer Night's Dream* and Amateur Performance', *Shakespeare Survey*, 56 (2003), 117–25.

Allen Dunn, 'The Indian Boy's Dream Wherein Every Mother's Son Rehearses His Part: Shakespeare's *A Midsummer Night's Dream*', *Shakespeare Studies*, 20 (1988), 15–32.

Stephen Fender, *A Midsummer Night's Dream*: Studies in English Literature, 35 (London: Arnold, 1968).

Henry Fenwick, 'The Production', in *BBC TV Shakespeare: A Midsummer Night's Dream* (London: British Broadcasting Corporation, 1981), pp. 18–26.

John R. Ford, 'Recounting Our Dreams: Imagining Shakespeare in Two Recent Film and Televised Adaptations of *A Midsummer Night's Dream*', *Shakespeare Bulletin* 26.3 (2008), 31–43.

Marjorie B. Garber, *Dream in Shakespeare: from metaphor to metamorphosis* (New Haven; London: Yale University Press, 1974).

Joshua Goldstein, *War and Gender: How Gender Shapes the War System and Vice-Versa* (Cambridge: Cambridge University Press, 2001).

Susanne Greenhalgh, 'Dream Children: Staging and Screening Childhood in *A Midsummer Night's Dream*', in Kate Chedgzoy, Susanne Greenhalgh and Robert Shaughnessy (eds), *Shakespeare and Childhood* (Cambridge: Cambridge University Press, 2007), pp. 201–17.

Weston A. Gui, 'Bottom's Dream', *American Image* 9 (1952), 251–305.

Andrew Gurr and Mariko Ichikawa, *Staging in Shakespeare's Theatres* (Oxford: Oxford University Press, 2000).

William Hazlitt, *Characters of Shakespeare's plays* (1817; London: Dent, 1906).

Margot Hendricks, '"Obscured by Dreams": Race, Empire and Shakespeare's *A Midsummer Night's Dream*', *Shakespeare Quarterly*, 47 (1996), 37–60.

Peter Holland, 'Theseus' Shadows in *A Midsummer Night's Dream*', *Shakespeare Survey*, 47 (1994), 137–51.

Tony Howard, 'Shakespeare on Film', *Source Guide* (British Film Institute, 2007), 1–2.

Russell Jackson, *Shakespeare Films in the Making: Vision, Production and Reception* (Cambridge: Cambridge University Press, 2007); see especially chapter 1.

Jack Jorgens, *Shakespeare on Film* (Bloomington: Indiana University Press, 1977). A pioneering and perceptive study.

Dennis Kennedy, *Granville Barker and the dream of theatre* (Cambridge: Cambridge University Press, 1985).

Dennis Kennedy, *Looking at Shakespeare: A Visual History of Twentieth-Century Performance* (Cambridge: Cambridge University Press, 2nd ed., 2001).

Frank Kermode, *Shakespeare's Language* (London: Penguin Books, 2000).

G. Wilson Knight, *The Shakespearean Tempest* (Oxford: Oxford University Press, 1932).

Jan Kott, 'Titania and the Ass's Head', in *Shakespeare Our Contemporary* (London: Methuen, 1965; reprinted 1983), pp. 171–90.

Jan Kott, 'Bottom and the Boys', *New Theatre Quarterly*, 9.36 (1993), 307–15.

Elliot Krieger, *A Marxist Study of Shakespeare's Comedies* (London: Macmillan, 1979), especially pp. 37–61; reprinted in Dutton 1996, pp. 38–60.

Steven F. Kruger, *Dreaming in the Middle Ages* (Cambridge: Cambridge University Press, 1992).

Mary Ellen Lamb, 'Taken by the Fairies: Fairy Practices and the Production of Popular Culture in *A Midsummer Night's Dream*', *Shakespeare Quarterly*, 51 (2000), 277–312.

Douglas Lanier, '"That You Have but Slumbered Here": A *Midsummer Night's Dream* in Popular Culture', in *A Midsummer Night's Dream: Shakespeare in Performance*, Advisory Editors, David Bevington and Peter Holland (London: A. C. Black, 2007), pp. 23–36.

François Laroque, *Shakespeare's Festive World: Elizabethan Seasonal Entertainment and the Professional Stage* (Cambridge: Cambridge University Press, 1991).

Minor White Latham, *The Elizabethan Fairie* (New York: Columbia University Press, 1930).

Theodore B. Leinwand, '"I believe we must leave the killing out": Deference and Accommodation in *A Midsummer Night's Dream*', *Renaissance Papers* (1986), 11–30.

A. Lewis, '*A Midsummer Night's Dream*: Fairy Fantasy or Erotic Nightmare', *Educational Theatre Journal*, 21.3 (1969), 251–58.

Glenn Loney, *Peter Brook's Production of William Shakespeare's A Midsummer Night's Dream for the Royal Shakespeare Company* (Stratford-upon-Avon: RSC, 1974). Prints the text as adapted for the production plus comments by Brook and some of the actors.

Michael MacOwan, 'The Sad Case of Professor Kott', *Drama*, 88 (Spring 1968), 30–7.

Christopher McCullough, 'Harley Granville Barker', in John Russell Brown (ed.), *The Routledge Companion to Directors' Shakespeare*, (London: Routledge, 2008), pp. 105–22.

Thomas McFarland, *Shakespeare's Pastoral Comedy* (Chapel Hill: University of North Carolina Press, 1972).

Moelwyn W. Merchant, '*A Midsummer Night's Dream*: A Visual Re-creation', in *Early Shakespeare* (eds), John Russell Brown and

Bernard Harris, Shakespeare Institute Studies (London: Arnold, 1961), 165–86.

Ronald F. Miller, 'A *Midsummer Night's Dream*: The Fairies, Bottom, and the Mystery of Things', *Shakespeare Quarterly*, 26 (1975), 254–68.

Louis A. Montrose, 'A Kingdom of Shadows', in Smith, Strier, Bevington, eds, 1995, pp. 68–86; incorporates some passages from his 1983 essay, 'Shaping Fantasies'.

Louis A. Montrose, '"Shaping Fantasies": Figurations of Gender and Power in Elizabethan Culture', *Representations*, 1 (1983), 61–94; reprinted in Dutton 1996, pp. 101–38.

Louis A. Montrose, 'A Kingdom of Shadows', in David L. Smith, Richard Strier and David Bevington (eds), *The Theatrical City: Culture, Theatre and Politics in London, 1576–1649* (Cambridge: Cambridge University Press, 1995), pp. 68–86; incorporates some passages from his 1983 essay, '"Shaping Fantasies"'.

Ruth Nevo, *Comic Transformations in Shakespeare* (London: Methuen, 1980).

Alfred Nutt, *The Fairy Mythology of Shakespeare* (New York: Haskill House Publishers, 1968).

A. D. Nuttall, 'A *Midsummer Night's Dream*: Comedy as *Apotrope* of Myth', *Shakespeare Survey* 53 (2000), 49–59.

Paul A. Olson, 'A *Midsummer Night's Dream* and the Meaning of Court Marriage', *English Literary History*, 24 (1957), 95–119; reprinted in abridged form in Price 1983, pp. 75–92. Olson argues that 'Commensurate with its origins in court marriage, this drama speaks throughout for a sophisticated Renaissance of the nature of love in both its rational and irrational forms' (pp. 95–6). Some will take exception to his view that Theseus and Hippolyta and their relationship from the start of the play represent order, but the essay offers a range of perceptive insights on the structure of the play.

Stephen Orgel, *Imagining Shakespeare* (Basingstoke: Palgrave Macmillan, 2003).

Patricia Parker, '(Peter) Quince: Love Potions, Carpenter's Coigns and Athenian Weddings', *Shakespeare Survey*, 56 (2003), 39–54.

Patricia Parker, 'Resistant readings, multilingualism and marginality' (with Calixto Bieito and Maria Delgado), in Lynette Hunter and Peter Lichtenfells (eds), *Shakespeare, Language and the Stage* (London: Thomson Learning, 2005).

Gail Paster and Skiles Howard (eds), *A Midsummer Night's Dream: Texts and Contexts* (Boston: Bedford, 1999).

Annabel Patterson, *Shakespeare and the Popular Voice* (Oxford: Blackwell, 1989). Reprinted in Smith 2004, pp. 220–41.

Michael Pennington, *A Midsummer Night's Dream: A User's Guide* (London: Nick Hern Books, 2005). An invaluable and enlightening study from the perspective of a performer/director.

Tom Pettitt, '"Perchance you wonder at this show": Dramaturgical Machinery in *A Midsummer Night's Dream*', in Philip Butterworth (ed.), *The Narrator, the Expositor, and the Prompter in European Medieval Theatre* (Turnhout, Belgium: Brepols, 2007), pp. 211–34.

William Rossky, 'Imagination in the English Renaissance: Psychology and Poetic', *Studies in the Renaissance*, 5 (1958), 49–73; extracts reprinted in Price 1983, pp. 93–9.

Kenneth S. Rothwell, *A History of Shakespeare on Screen: A Century of Film and Television* (Cambridge: Cambridge University Press, second edition, 2004).

Augustus W. Schlegel, *A Course of Lectures on Dramatic Art and Literature*, trans. John Black (London: Henry G. Bohn, 1846).

Kathryn Schwarz, *Tough Love: Amazon Encounters in the English Renaissance* (Durham: Duke University Press, 2000).

David Selbourne, *The Making of A Midsummer Night's Dream: An Eyewitness Account of Peter Brook's Production from First Rehearsal to First Night* (London: Methuen, 1982).

Alan Sinfield, 'Cultural Materialism and Intertextuality: The Limits of Queer Reading in *A Midsummer Night's Dream* and *The Two Noble Kinsmen*', *Shakespeare Quarterly*, 56 (2003), 67–78.

David L. Smith, Richard Strier, David Bevington (eds), *The Theatrical City: Culture, Theatre and Politics in London 1576–1649* (Cambridge: Cambridge University Press, 1995).

John Sutherland and Cedric Watts, *Henry V, War Criminal? & Other Shakespeare Puzzles* (Oxford: Oxford University Press, 2000).

A. B. Taylor, '"When Everything Seems Double": Peter Quince, the Other Playwright in *A Midsummer Night's Dream*', *Shakespeare Survey*, 56 (2003), 55–66.

Leonard Tennenhouse, 'Strategies of State and Political Plays: *A Midsummer Night's Dream, Henry IV, Henry V, Henry VIII*', in Jonathan Dollimore and Alan Sinfield (eds), *Political Shakespeare: New Essays* in *Cultural Materialism* (Manchester: Manchester University Press, 1985), pp. 109–28.

Keith Thomas, *Religion and the Decline of Magic: Studies in Popular Beliefs in Sixteenth and Seventeenth Century England* (Harmondsworth: Penguin, 1973).

Keith Thomas, *Man and the Natural World: Changing Attitudes in England 1500–1800* (Harmondsworth: Penguin, 1983).

Peter Thomson, *Shakespeare's Professional Career* (Cambridge: Cambridge University Press, pb. ed., 1999).

R. Larry Todd, *Mendelssohn: A Life in Music* (Oxford: Oxford University Press, 2003).

Herbert Beerbohm Tree, *Thoughts and After-Thoughts* (London: Cassell, 1913).

Brian Vickers, *The Artistry of Shakespeare's Prose* (London: Methuen, 1968).

Wendy Wall, 'Why Does Puck Sweep? Fairylore, Merry Wives, and Social Struggle', *Shakespeare Quarterly*, 52 (2001), 70–106.

Roger Warren, *A Midsummer Night's Dream: Text and Performance* (London: Macmillan, 1983).

Ronald Watkins and Jeremy Lemmon, *In Shakespeare's Playhouse: A Midsummer Night's Dream* (London: David & Charles, 1974).

Robert Weimann, *Author's Pen and Actor's Voice: Playing and Writing in Shakespeare's Theatre* (Cambridge: Cambridge University Press, 2000).

Stanley Wells, *Shakespeare for All Time* (London: Macmillan, 2002).

Martin White, *Renaissance Drama in Action: An Introduction to Aspects of Theatre Practice and Performance* (London: Routledge, 1998).

Glynne Wickham, 'A *Midsummer Night's Dream*: The Setting and the Text', in *Shakespeare's Dramatic Heritage* (London: Routledge & Kegan Paul, 1969).

David Wiles, *Shakespeare's Almanac: A Midsummer Night's Dream, Marriage and the Elizabethan Calendar* (Cambridge: D. S. Brewer, 1993).

David Wiles, 'The Carnivalesque in *A Midsummer Night's Dream*', in Ronald Knowles (ed.), *Shakespeare and Carnival: After Bakhtin* (Basingstoke: Macmillan, 1998), pp. 61–82.

Gary J. Williams, *Our Moonlight Revels: A Midsummer Night's Dream in the Theatre* (Iowa City: University of Iowa Press, 1997). Indispensible; the most comprehensive performance history of the play that places each production in its cultural and historical moment.

Penny Williams, 'Social Tensions Contained', in Smith, Strier, Bevington (eds), 1995, 55–67.

Robert F. Willson, Jr, *Shakespeare in Hollywood, 1929–1956* (London: Associated University Presses, 2000). The chapter on the Reinhardt/Dieterle film is particularly helpful in setting the film, its conventions, casting and reception in the context of the Hollywood film industry in the 1930s.

John Dover Wilson, *Shakespeare's Happy Comedies* (London: Faber and Faber, 1962).

Richard Wilson, 'The Kindly Ones: The Death of the Author in Shakespearean Athens', in Dutton, 1996, 198–222.

David P. Young, *Something of Great Constancy: the Art of A Midsummer Night's Dream* (New Haven, CT: Yale University Press, 1966).

Index